Doctor Zhivago & an anatomy of a Revolution

ANNA MATZOV

Copyright © 2015 Anna Matzov

All rights reserved.

ISBN-13: 978-1517525842
ISBN-10: 1517525845

The lack of skill to find and tell the truth is a shortcoming for which no talent can cover up.

—Boris Pasternak

◆ ◆ ◆

The content of a novel could not become itself without technique, and it becomes what it is because it has been caught in a particular way; the artistic worth of a novel resides largely in its being caught in the one way inevitable to it …

… This principle of uniqueness implies that every work of art is created and should be judged by its own rules; it must grow its particular form as a snail its shell, not like a hermit crab that adjusts itself to the abandoned shell of another creature.

—A.A. Mendilow

Contents

Introduction ... iv

Revealing the Structural Code of the Chapter Titles

1	Part One: The Five O'Clock Express	1
2	A Girl From a Different Circle	11
3	Christmas Party at the Sventitskys	17
4	The Imminent and the Inevitable	23
5	Farewell to the Past	27
6	Moscow Bivouac	33
7	The Journey (On the Road)	37
8	Part Two: Arrival	47
9	Varykino	53
10	The Highway	63
11	Forest Brotherhood	71
12	Iced Rowanberries	75
13	Opposite the House of Caryatids	81
14	Again Varykino	87

Contents

| 15 | Conclusion (The End) | 93 |
| 16 | The Epilogue | 99 |

Skaz and Stream of Consciousness	103
Point of View in the Novel	131
Sources	160

Introduction

In this novel, without hyperbole or political rhetoric, the history and the fundamental realities that were the results of the Great October Revolution are laid bare.

Doctor Zhivago is an impressionistic rendering of idealistic hopes turned into a realistic revolution. Written in a poetic, symbolic style, with a clear strategy to avoid didacticism, the novel becomes a formula for understanding the seeds and results of not just the Russian October Revolution but of any revolution.

In the heat of the cold war over half a century ago Boris Pasternak's novel *Doctor Zhivago* was published abroad, in Italy. At a time when the Socialist Realism doctrine dominated literature in the Soviet Union, *Doctor Zhivago* was the first work of a Soviet writer to be published abroad before it was approved and published in the Soviet Union. Moreover, in this novel Pasternak dared to write about the October Revolution, the Civil War and life in the Soviet state the way they truly were, not the way they were presented in the dogmatic Social Realism literature. Thus, the first hole was drilled in the ominous iron curtain, and the first look into the reality behind it was in focus! The most apolitical of Soviet poets became a political traitor at home and a hero abroad. The scandal the novel created in the Soviet Union and the antagonism among different political critics in the West made an unbiased understanding and evaluation of the novel virtually impossible.

What makes the reading and study of the novel so momentous is the fact that over fifty-eight years since the novel's publication, with all the political changes that have taken place in the world since, the issues deliberated in the novel are still ever so relevant and will continue to be relevant.

Pasternak felt it was his obligation to write this novel and to tell what he considered to be the truth, an act which—due to the regime he lived under—he postponed for many years. *Doctor Zhivago* is a Russian novel; everything that happens in it takes place in Russia and the characters are for the most part Russian. But what made and still makes the novel so germane is that Pasternak's observations of the events and characters are of such a universal spirit that they could easily apply to another place and another time. One can read the novel as the nature of revolution versus evolution, of truth compared to un-truth, or real life in contrast to false propaganda about life.

Doctor Zhivago was not the first try for Pasternak to write a novel as a vehicle to tell the truth as he perceived it. When in the early thirties of the last century it became impossible to publish literature without Soviet propaganda, some writers became silent; others cooperated with the regime and wrote fiction to please it. Only a very few managed to write without succumbing to the demands of the regime. Pasternak was one of the latter few. For many years he did not compromise his honesty. In disharmony of his poetry with the regime, he supported himself and his family by translating great works of the classics. He left his mark in his creative translations of Goethe's Faust, many of Shakespeare's works, Georgian works of poetry and more. From the beginning of his writing life he strongly believed that truth is a mandatory element of a work of art. In order for a work to have artistic value, it has to convey the truth of the issue it places under review. Even more, it has to seek the right position, the just point of view, the apt metaphor and all it needs to find and tell the truth.

When Pasternak started his novel, writing about what life really was in Russia and not adhering to the ideological formula of Socialist Realism could get him into precarious predicaments. The Communist Party found out early—already in the 1920s—that literature could be a useful tool to realize its goals. At the time when Pasternak was writing his novel, as for three decades, real life in Russia was not reflected in its literature. Facts and reality were replaced in literature with works that followed the dogmatic formula of Socialist Realism. This new life was glorified in the local media and abroad by an extremely well organized propaganda machine, which also appropriated a role to the enormous production of literature in the spirit of Socialist Realism. Soviet life, as described according to the Socialist Realism formula, was respected and admired, not only by naive Soviet readers, but also by many gullible readers in countries outside the Soviet Union. Many sympathizers viewed the Soviet Union as the greatest achievement in human history, as the most successful political system ever known to man. Inside and outside the Soviet Union, the Soviet regime was held in high esteem by many intellectuals and proletarians alike.

According to his correspondence, Pasternak wrote *Doctor Zhivago* for those members of the Russian public who belonged to his generation, for those who read and loved his poetry and his early prose. He felt indebted to them for their trust in him and their admiration of his work. In order to live up to their trust, he felt he owed it to them and to history to tell the true story about the generation he and they belonged to, to tell it the way he experienced and understood it. His readers came from all walks of Russian life and Pasternak wanted his message to reach as many of them as he could. Hence the novel had to be written in as simple a style as possible, in a style different from his previous works, in a form accessible to all. When he started to write the novel, the illusions of any semblance of freedom that appeared during WWII, had already vanished and the 'cold war' was at the height of its momentum. Thus there was no hope to have the novel published in the Soviet Union and certainly not even a thought of having it published abroad. He wrote it 'for the drawer', as they used to say at the time. He submitted the novel to the members of the editorial board of *Novyi Mir*, who kept their opinion to themselves until he was awarded the Novel Prize. Then, when an outright and terrible war was declared against Pasternak in the press, they too published a lengthy critical article, arguing why it could not be published.

Since not even the 'drawer' was a completely safe place, Pasternak employed a number of devices to deliver his message. Those for whom the work was written deciphered the hints in the text more easily than did the uninitiated. For example, the appearance of the church of Christ the Savior in two places in the novel, the first time when Yurii arrives in Moscow from the West (from Meluzeevo) and the second time when he comes from the East (from Varykino) to Moscow, did not get my attention in spite of several careful readings of the novel, since at the time I lacked specific knowledge of what happened to this church by Stalin's orders. Only when I re-read the novel after Perestroika started and when the rebuilding of the church became a popular issue, did I notice its presence and role in the text. (At the time Pasternak was writing the novel, there was no church there; it had been blown up and was replaced by the world's largest swimming pool.) I am sure that there are many more examples in the text of such seemingly cryptic hidden phenomena which I have missed and which were more easily spotted by readers to whom this work primarily was directed.

My work does not focus on the politics or the history of the novel's publication. However, in order to shed light on and understand in the text some subtleties and intimations, which will be discussed here, the political climate that prevailed at the time the novel was written cannot be ignored. A clearer understanding and sense of conditions of the time is rendered in Cingiz Aitmatov's novel *And the Day Lasts Longer than a Century* (title not incidentally taken from Pasternak's poem).

    Considering Pasternak's other works and the ideas about style that the protagonist of the novel espouses, one cannot help but think that Pasternak's beliefs and skills were invested to achieve what he thought to be a 'clear and simple style.' The generation for whom he wrote it most probably could understand the cues and metaphors better than readers who were complete strangers to the reality of the life described in the novel. It is my hope that an attentive reading of the novel—as shown in my work—with more awareness and understanding of the method Pasternak used to convey his message, will not only deepen the understanding of the novel, but also open up to the reader an important aspect of the content, which is imparted through the very form of the novel.

♦ ♦ ♦

    As often happens with a work of art that is dictated by its author's conscience, beliefs and sense of duty to convey what he considers the truth, the novel is replete with symbols, metaphors and every possible device to communicate the messages the author wishes to convey. I lay no claim to have found them all; I am sure many such hidden references that I have missed will be unveiled by others. Believing that some of the novel's messages are lost in translation, I have focussed most of my attention on the content expressed in form in the original Russian text. For instance, the role that the titles of the chapters play is more salient in Russian than in translation. Moreover, in some other cases the Russian original text delivers a message which is completely lost in translation.

    Regardless how we approach the novel, an objective inquisitive reading—if such a thing is at all possible—reveals that there is well-founded reason to expect that the value that this work of literature holds in our world today will endure into future times.

It may help us to recognize and become more alert to the danger of the empty word when it occurs. The same forces that lead the Russian Enlightenment to the October Revolution and to the cruel and catastrophic changes in people like Pasha Antipow, his father, Tiverzin and others, who corrupted by power and hatred become mass murderers, appeared and will continue to appear in other societies as well. As shown in this novel, the powers that make history are certainly not confined to the time described here or to Russia alone.

As realized in his short life, the philosophy about life, art and history of the protagonist, Yurii Zhivago, inspired by his uncle Nikolay Vedeniapin, is the antithesis of the philosophy and actions of the contemporary revolutionaries. Thus, one of the central issues of the novel is the predicament of the individual in a revolutionary world and, as we have learned since, it is not limited to Yurii's time in history or his place in the world.

It needs emphasizing that the novel offers much more than what my work brings to the table. What overwhelmed me in my first reading of the novel and what made me go back and study it, is the very spirit of the novel. It tells a story about the strength and importance of inner freedom in validating an individual's life. The protagonist of the novel, Yurii Zhivago, is a free individual; he forms his own opinion of the historical time in which he lives and he does not abdicate to the considerable and pervasive external pressures of his time. He loses his family, his greatest love and his life. But his poems, like this novel, free of the language and didactics of his time, are an inspiration not only to his friends but to all those who at any and all times seek freedom.

In reading the novel many may find the power of the love story—one of the 20th century greatest—stirring and irresistible to the point that it may overshadow many other issues. Some find the poems, the last chapter of the novel, and the description of the writing of some of the poems an original and valuable lesson in both writing and reading poetry. But what first and foremost preserves the great importance of this novel and makes it viable also today is the fact that it tells about the Individual in a Revolutionary world, after fifty-eight years still as relevant a story as ever.

The Bolshevik Revolution did not function. Soviet life after the Revolution was not what the Soviet propaganda labored to have the world believe. This message, clear on several levels in *Doctor Zhivago*, is expressed also in other, dystopian, works, e.g., *We* by Zamiatin, written in 1921, as well as Orwell's *1984*, written in 1948 (when Pasternak was already two years into the writing of *Doctor Zhivago)*. Orwell was inspired by Zamiatin and both were inspired by the same experiment of Soviet reality. The emphasis on regimented and controlled life in these works, however, is alleviated in *Doctor Zhivago* with the celebration of life in its fullness; the highs, the lows and everything in between, create a full picture of life. Moreover, despite the terrible times described in the text, the novel is an ode to Life with capital L.

The battle of words, as used by both political antagonists in the novel, the propaganda machine and—in the midst of this havoc—Zhivago's poetry instill in us in the end the belief that time is a judge to be trusted and that truth and historical justice will be victorious.

My centre of attention has been to bring into the open Boris Pasternak's brilliant use of form in *Doctor Zhivago* to express content and I have sought to highlight and treasure the spirit and values imparted by the novel, some of which are in plain text and others in subtle form.

Revealing the Structural Code of the Chapter Titles

PART ONE

CHAPTER ONE: THE FIVE O'CLOCK EXPRESS

On the following pages we will see how the titles of the chapters can direct the way the text is read. The title helps us notice and understand the way the author connects ideas, events and other categories of life, which are scattered in a subtle form throughout the text. To show the method used we will first concentrate on the technique Pasternak uses to express only one of the principal ideas of this chapter. I will italicize those parts of the text which make it easier to follow those events and phenomena that show the connectedness between the title and the text. The issues discussed in this chapter are from two levels of existence: those regarded as 'natural' (given to observation and rational explanation) and the metaphysical (that which cannot be seen or explained in the same terms).

The argument taking place between Nikolay Nikolayevich Vedenyapin and Ivan Ivanovich Voskoboynikov is on the level of what we perceive as 'natural.' Vedenyapin, the bearer of the spiritual values in the novel, gets carried away by his philosophical ideas and talks to Voskoboynikov about the meaning of immortality and the teachings of Christ. Voskoboynikov, a pragmatist and rationalist, believes only in practical solutions to the problems of life—such as the solutions to the peasants' plight—and that solutions are to be found in agrarian reforms and other pragmatic approaches. He tries to interrupt Vedenyapin by changing the topic. When this does not work, however, he stops their argument with the following words: "That's metaphysics, my dear fellow. It's forbidden me by my doctors, my stomach won't take it" (p. 19).

The argument between them is left unresolved on the rational level of existence. The coincidence in time and space of Yurii's father's death and Yurii's fainting, however, could be seen as an indirect answer to their argument on another level of existence, on a level beyond the rational, beyond the understandable. The author does not mention a connection between these two events, neither does he make the participants of the discussion aware of the two events that take place simultaneously with their discussion. However, it looks like Pasternak uses this first coincidence in time and space as affirmation of consonance of their attitude vis-à-vis metaphysics. If this 'casual' time-space coincidence draws the observant reader's attention, it is only when the reader tries to understand the connection between the title and the text.

This is the first of many time-space coincidences in the plot of the novel. It should be mentioned here that, while many other coincidences were often pointed out as 'structural flaws' by early critics of the novel, this particular coincidence was never discussed before. For some reason, this coincidence is not considered important at first glance and does not play a dynamic role in the structure or content of the plot (at the 'natural' level) as those often discussed by critics. Actually, it should be pointed out that this coincidence was detected while considering the title ('The Five O'Clock Express') of a chapter full of so many important details of life in Russia. Thus, it seems that the title here has a structural function; it is designed to direct the reader's attention to events or facts that are supposedly secondary to the content of the story.

The fourth section of this chapter describes the arrival of Yurii and Vedenyapin in Duplanka. While Vedenyapin and Voskoboynikov are absorbed with editing the work that Vedenyapin brought with him to Voskoboynikov, Yurii sets out to look for Nika around the house. At the end of the fifth chapter we encounter the train:

> "Fancy, it's only just gone five," said Ivan Ivanovich. "There is the express from Syzran. *It comes through here a few minutes after five.*"
>
> Far out on the plain, crossing it from right to left, came a neat little yellow and blue train, made tiny by the distance. Suddenly they saw that it had stopped. White puffs of steam flurried over the engine and a moment later they heard its alarmed hooting.
>
> "That's strange," said Voskoboynikov. "Something is wrong. *It has no business to stop in the middle of the marsh out there.* Something must have happened. Let's go and have tea" (p. 20).

From this passage we learn that the five o'clock express stops at the *marsh* and that the time is *a few minutes after five.* They are going to have tea, and before going toward the house, Nikolay Nikolayevich calls Yurii, who has gone to look for Nika. Yurii does not find Nika, as we are told in the next chapter. Beautiful nature, flowers, birds and the gully remind Yurii of places he had visited with his deceased mother. The memory of his mother makes Yurii pray:

> "Angel of God, my holy guardian," Yurii prayed ... "Lord, and please don't let her suffer. Mama," in his heart-rending anguish he called her down from heaven like a newly canonised saint and suddenly, unable to bear any more, *fell down in a faint.*

He was not unconscious for long. When he came to himself, he heard his uncle calling him from above. He answered and started climbing out of the gully. Suddenly he remembered that he had not prayed for his missing father, as his mother had taught him to do.

... and it occurred to him that nothing much would happen if he prayed for his father another time (p. 21).

The time sequence of events is the following: Yurii's uncle and Voskoboynikov notice that the train stops at exactly a *few minutes after five;* immediately after this, Voskoboynikov asks Nikolay Nikolayevich to return to the house for tea; not having seen Yurii until then, Nikolay Nikolayevich calls out for him; Yurii, who is not unconscious for long, comes to his senses as he hears his uncle's voice; it seems that *the train stops and Yurii faints at the same time!* (or within minutes, at the most).

The next chapter describes what is taking place around the train. *The suicide of Yurii's father is the reason the train stops.* A description of the view from the opposite side (from the train) confirms that it is the same train Voskoboynikov and Vedenyapin see from Duplanka:

All the passengers came out and had a look at the corpse ...
As they jumped out on the track ... they felt as if the whole place had only been brought into being by the halt and that neither the *squelchy marsh nor the broad river nor the fine house and church* on the steep bank opposite would have existed except for the accident (p. 24).

Earlier Voskoboynikov mentions the *marsh* when he says there is no reason for the train to stop. And before that he also mentions the river: " 'Let's go down to the river while they are getting tea ready,' suggested Ivan Ivanovich" (p. 18). Amplifying the importance of the place, we find the same elements of the Kologrivov estate one more time in Yurii's memory of it: '[H]e expected the road to turn right and give a fleeting view of the Kologrivov estate with its ten-mile stretch of open country, *the river gleaming in the distance and the railway beyond it'* (p. 16).

The minute and repeated details of the locality, seen through the eyes of Voskoboynikov, Vedenyapin, Yurii and the train passengers, are meant to bring to the reader's attention this first time-space coincidence (in the same space and the same time).The meaning of Andrei Zhivago's death and his son Yurii's fainting at the same time in the same space is an answer from beyond the text to an argument taking place in the text.

By presenting information leading to this coincidence in a scattered form, leaving the symbolically presented argument between Nikolay Nikolayevich and Ivan Ivanovich unresolved in the plain of 'natural' events, and introducing an 'irrational' coincidence as a possible answer on a different plane, introducing in this way an additional perception of existence to include occurrences not given to rational explanations already in the opening chapter of the novel, Pasternak validates Nikolay Nikolayevich's theories tacitly, without words. On a structural level, the title encourages the reader to look for less obvious details and, as we see in this case, to discover a subtext beyond the printed word.

Thus, the above structure of the text can be seen here as a poetic device employed to convey a certain kind of information in a different form, available to the reader according to level of interest. While being outside the story, its message is important. For the attentive reader this additional content organizes and shapes a higher level of understanding of the 'reality' portrayed in the novel. The attention drawn to the chronology of the meeting—to be at the same time and the same place—is attained here by describing the location several times from different directions as viewed through the eyes of various people. The time is stated precisely and only once. It is five o'clock, the same time that Yurii faints and his father dies.

It is definitely the title that leads the reader to look for the above details which otherwise would be easily missed. Since this opening presents the reader with many of the major ideological issues of the novel, it helps to be alerted already in the beginning to the main philosophical issues on which the novel touches.

The novel opens with the first funeral (there are two more to follow), seen from outside by the passersby:

On they went, singing 'Eternal Memory,' and whenever they stopped, their feet, the horses, and the gusts of wind seemed to carry their singing.

Passersby made way for the procession, *counted the wreaths, and crossed themselves.* Some joined in out of curiosity and asked: "Who is being buried?"— "Zhivago," they were told. — "Oh, I see. That's what it is." — "It isn't him. It's his wife." — "Well, it comes to the same thing. *May her soul rest in peace. It's a fine* [ric h, AM] *funeral"* (p. 13).

This funeral is defined by the song the people in the procession are singing, and by the passersby who are counting the wreaths and crossing themselves. Their behaviour shows them to be in awe of both riches and death. The emphasis on counting the wreaths, crossing themselves, voicing "May she rest in peace" and concluding that it is a rich funeral confirms that they react to wealth and death with awe and innate fear.

Considering that all this takes place to the sounds of singing 'Eternal Memory,' the ultimate achievement of mortals, it is possible to conclude that the author juxtaposes the above common human features—to be in awe of riches and death—with the highest noble realization of a mortal, eternal memory.

The fact that this short chapter ends with Yurii, the protagonist of the novel, being led out of the graveyard by a priest who has left the church by his own choice, symbolically confirms the author's antagonistic position regarding conventions, including the procedure at the funeral described here. Even so, later in the novel, at the Soviet-style funeral for Yurii, Lara's nostalgia for a church funeral will appear in the text.

In the following section we find Yurii and his uncle spending the first night after the funeral in a monastery. Woken by a storm, the child sees in it threatening consequences for the graveyard, beds of cabbages and more: 'Yurii's first impulse was to dress, run outside and start doing something' (p. 14). This reaction should be remembered as we follow the development of Yurii's character.

In the next section we learn about Yurii's parents, his childhood ('This way, in disorder and among constant riddles, passed the childhood years of the child's life, often left with strangers who often changed' (p. 15) and the road from riches to poverty. The sad facts of life were hidden from Yurii.

Section four touches upon the situation of the peasants, the landowners and the pragmatic and philosophical approach to the problems in the countryside.

In a short dialogue between Nikolay Nikolayevich and Pavel we learn that the peasants and even progressive people like Vedenyapin perceive ownership of land differently. The resistance of some peasants to the existing law and order in the country is seen by Pavel as a transgression that has to be stopped brutally, the old way.

In this section Vedenyapin is introduced as the author of books that are not yet written, but are soon to appear. As a man who, except for the terminology, would not have anything in common with the intellectuals of his time, 'He craved for an idea, inspired yet concrete, that would change the world for the better, an idea as unmistakable, even to a child or ignorant fool, as lightning or a roll of thunder. He craved for something new' (p. 17). His uncle reminds Yurii of his mother, who '[l]ike hers, his mind moved with freedom and was open to the unfamiliar. He had the same aristocratic sense of equality with all living things ...' (p. 17).

Unlike Pavel, Vedenyapin believes in equality of all people.

In part five we are exposed to the differences of beliefs accompanied by the differences of style which distinguish Nikolay Nikolayevich from Ivan Ivanovich Voskoboynikov. The erudite Vedenyapin tells Voskoboynikov about the situation in the country. 'The truth is only sought by individuals, and they break with those who do not love it enough' (p. 18). In less than two pages Vedenyapin conveys all his ideas about Christ, immortality, life, history and much more, which Voskoboynikov, the pragmatist, sees as metaphysics, of no interest to him. His materialistic ideology stops at schools and hospitals for the peasants.

Part six gives us an idea of Yurii's religious beliefs and prayers. Is his childish perception of 'life after death' typical or not for a Russian child of his class at the time? Or is it characteristic of Yurii Zhivago to address God, as we read also about his later life?

Part seven offers a glimpse at the passengers of the train that stopped across the river. Misha Gordon, who is travelling with his father, and who will be one of Yurii's closest friends, is representing the predicament of Jews in Russia. The crowd is generalized by their happiness and assuredness of the existence of God. The Gordons become friendly with Andrei Zhivago and Grigory Osipovich, Misha's father, tries unsuccessfully to prevent Zhivago's suicide. The train is stopped by Grigory Gordon. Three Tiverzin women are on the train and pray by the corpse. The procedure of handling the case, the response of the crowd to the long waiting for the train to start and other behaviour provide a symbolic picture of the social composition of the travellers as a microcosm of the stratification of society in the country. Last but not least, Komarovsky is introduced as the possible cause of Andrei Zhivago's despair and suicide.

In the last section of this chapter Nicky Dudorov, the second friend of Yurii's, represents the revolutionary Russia. His parents are both revolutionaries: his father, convicted for inciting terror, is far away, and his mother, a Georgian princess, is dedicated to the revolution and neglects her much-loved son. Nika is staying at the Kologrivov estate together with their daughters and Voskoboynikov, the educator. We finish the first chapter with a romantic encounter of two teenagers. This scene of first love is drawn as by a few brushstrokes in watercolour.

By the time the scene with the train comes into the story, many of the characters, ideas and issues have been already introduced. The title of the chapter hardly seems a logical choice at this point. Did the author expect the readers to look for an explanation? Did he expect that in search of an answer the reader would pay attention to all kind of details and would notice the time-space coincidence? Further examination of the novel shows the enormous role the title plays in directing the reader's attention toward certain details which would be missed without this structural device. It is, in fact, through these details that the content of the novel extends beyond the printed text.

CHAPTER TWO:
A GIRL FROM A DIFFERENT CIRCLE

    This chapter introduces in the novel the second plot line which is led by Lara Guishar. By referring in the title to her circle as different, the contrast between Lara's milieu of family, friends and acquaintances and the one in which Yurii grows up is highlighted. The title makes us look back and compare the different circles we are introduced to. And it is due to the title that, without being mentioned, the people around Lara are contrasted with those described in the first chapter around Yurii.
    The encounter between these ambits, the first indirect meeting of Yurii and Lara, the protagonists of the two plot lines, is accompanied by showing the extreme conditions of their environments: straight from the opulent atmosphere of a home concert in the Gromeko living room we are moved to the moral filth of the Montenegro hotel. The choice of language, dialogue and characters shows that people are defined not by who they are but by the milieu into which they seem to be born.

  Egorovna muttered in his ear.
    "What Montenegro?"
    "The hotel."
    "Well, what about it?"
    "They're asking for him to come at once. *There's somebody of yours* [i.e., 'your class'] dying."
    So now they're dying! I can't imagine. It can't be done, Yegorovna. When they will finish that piece I'll tell him. Until then I can't."

"They have sent a waiter with a cab to fetch him. Somebody is dying, I tell you, can't you understand? *It's a lady, one of the gentry*" (p. 60).

"And who's the one that all the fuss is about now, I ask you? You'd think somebody worth smashing crockery for. But it's *that slut, that street walker giving herself airs, that madam-five-bob-a-time, innocence in retirement ...*" (p. 62).

It all turned out quite differently from anything Alexander Alexandrovich had expected. *He had imagined a clean and dignified tragedy in a musician's life*. But this was the devil of a business. *Sordid and scandalous, and certainly not for children* (p. 62).

Humour and irony are rendered in the dialogue through the choice of vocabulary and the reaction of different social voices to the same event. Each one of them relates to the event from her or his own point of view, from her or his position in society, reflecting the 'circle' to which she or he belongs. Moreover, each one of them sees the same Guishar as a member of a different circle. For Yegorovna she belongs to 'your people' (speaking to Gromeko, who belongs to the gentry). For the hotel employees, who are used to seeing the dwellers of this hotel in a different light, she is 'madam-five-bob-a-time' and other characteristics of the same category. Gromeko is disappointed that the reasons for her attempted suicide were not 'clean and dignified.' The three voices are completely isolated from each other, the same way the milieus they represent are. Obviously, there is no dialogue taking place between them in the text. Each description ascribed to Guishar, however, reflects the speaker's place in society. Consequently, this almost abstract presentation of the situation evokes an ironic notion regarding the conventional way of looking at a person through a filter of 'circumstantial characteristics'—seeing a person as part of a group of people rather than as an individual.

The above incident is one of many metaphors, this one a presentation of the phenomenon of circles. There are many other situations presented in this chapter that are metaphors for the dynamics of the coexistence of and interaction between the representatives of these and many other ambits in Russian society of the time:

- Komarovsky and the Guishars.
- The railway and the different groups involved in its functioning: Antipov, Tiverzin, Fuflygin: The administration.
- Khudoleev, Yusupka: Ethnic issues.
- The political movements and persons involved in the perceptions of the situation in the country from the railroad worker's point of view (chapters 6, 7, 8); more faces, more names never to be seen again (chapter 9).

It is not coincidental that the majority of the existing spheres are introduced in the first two chapters of the novel. Sometimes they are represented just by a name, which is often mentioned only once. (I suspect that the reason for these names being mentioned is obscure to most of those readers who are unfamiliar with old Moscow or the origins of the names, and this might also be the reason that some of them were left out in the English translation.) The list of names follows: the Vedenyapins; the Ostromyslenskys; the Seliavins; the Michaelises; the Sventitskys; and the Gromekos (relations of Yurii's in Moscow) (section 20 in Russian original). The different guests at the Gromeko concert (left out in the English translation) are Adelaida Filipovna, Gintz (different from the one in chapter three), the Fufukovs, the Basurmans, the Verzhitskys, Colonel Kavkaztsev, Shura Shlesinger, and the concert performers. Other names include the Guishars, Demina, the Tiverzins, the Antipovs, the Fuflygins, the hotel staff, Tyshkevich, Voskoboynikov, Kologrivov, Gordons, Vyvolochnov, Khudoleyev and many others.

Without having researched the origins of every one of these names, I believe that the reason they appear here is to remind Pasternak's generation of the old names, before they were changed to Soviet ones (for example, Skriabin became Molotov and Ulyanov became Lenin), or to preserve in mind the names of people who left the country.

It is the structural function of the title that can justify this long list of names and that highlights the convention of dividing people into certain categories at this time. It is important to notice that dividing people into circles, or classes, will be shown to continue after the revolution as well.

The idea of the free individual is one of the main themes of the novel. Perceiving a person through the characteristics of a milieu, class or other group—which, to start with, is often not a person's own choice—is as old a convention as recorded human history itself. Hence it is not surprising that all throughout the novel, parallel to the main theme of the free individual, runs the motif of the convention to divide people by categorization. This division is seen as one of the major forces acting against the free individual. This convention changes its appearance with time; the criteria of division change but the division persists and continues to be directed against the free individual. Thus, again, the title highlights the main issues discussed in this chapter—an issue that is present in all places and at all times.

The concluding coincidence of this chapter describes a meeting of people from different backgrounds: Komarovsky, Misha Gordon, Gromeko, Tyshkevich, Lara and Yurii find themselves in the same, most unexpected, place. Each of them belongs to a different ambit, due to their social or ethnic origin. It is also worth noticing that it is here that Yurii sees Lara for the first time. This is the first meeting of the protagonists of the great love story of the novel. Yurii sees Lara interacting with Komarovsky; their relationship is a riddle to him. He senses something he never felt before. He is mesmerized by the girl but does not yet understand the feelings she provokes in him. The class difference seems not to exist at the level of natural human attraction.

CHAPTER THREE:
CHRISTMAS PARTY AT THE SVENTITSKYS

In this chapter, only two of the seventeen sections bring up the Christmas party; also, several important themes and dynamic motifs of the plot are developed here. Why then assign the title to two out of seventeen sections? It is true that it is at this party that Lara, Yurii, Komarovsky and Tonya are brought under one roof. (Only Yurii knows all the others.) Lara comes here without being invited. She comes to shoot Komarovsky and instead slightly wounds the public prosecutor.

The Christmas party serves as a junction in which plot lines dealing with several themes intersect. The evening attire in which Yurii and Tonya appear in front of Anna Ivanovna were made for the party. Lara arrives at the party to settle her score with Komarovsky. The streets of Moscow, which the protagonists pass on their way to the party, play a symbolic role here and are portrayed twice. Once they are seen with Lara's eyes on the way to Komarovsky's:

'She walked through the festive streets in a terrible excitement, seeing nothing, not aware of anything ...' (p. 78).

Then, not finding Komarovsky at home and heading to the *Christmas party*, she continues her search for him. On her way to the party she starts to notice the festive streets of the city:

Only now, when she came out for the second time, did she take a look around her at the town and the winter night.

> *Screened with a crust of ice and snow, the windows of the houses were chalk white, and the coloured reflections of lighted Christmas trees and shadows of merrymakers moved across their opaque surface as if a magic lantern show were being given in the street* (p. 78).

The second time, the festive street is described the way Yurii sees it. (Like in the case of Lara, the description of the state of mind precedes the visual perception of the street.)

> Yurii looked round and saw what Lara had seen a little earlier ... *The lights shining through the frosted windows turned the house into precious caskets of smoky topaz. Inside them glowed the Christmas life of Moscow, candles burned on trees, guests milled around and fooling about mummers were playing hide-and-seek and hunt-the-ring* (p. 81).

Yurii sees *the very same scene* as Lara; their inner world is reflected in their visions but the *festive streets* are highlighted by being the catalyst of these visions.

The Christmas atmosphere reverts Yurii's mind back to Blok and the article he promised to write about him:

> It occurred to him that *Blok is the phenomenon of Christmas in all areas of Russian life,* in the life of the northern city and in the newest in literature, underneath the starry skies of the contemporary street and around the lighted tree of this century's drawing-room. *There was no need to write an article on Blok,* he thought, *all you needed do was to paint a Russian version of a Dutch adoration of the Magi with snow in it, and wolves and a dark fir forest* (p. 81).

In Pasternak's short biography, in which he rates Blok's realism very highly, he writes:

... and how this style went well with the *spirit of the times*, which was lurking, concealed, underground, which barely came out from the cellars, which spoke the language of conspirators, whose principal face was the city, main event was the street.

And farther on, 'Reality's features, like by the stream of air, are noted down by the vortex of Blok's impressionability into his books'.
The festive streets of Moscow on Christmas Eve and the nature of the Christmas party at the Sventitskys are signs of an era which symbolically associate the atmosphere of Christmas with the times of Blok.
This chapter ends with Anna Ivanovna's funeral. Along with her, the author buries an epoch. The Christmas Eve on Moscow streets, the Christmas party at the Sventitskys, the church funeral service—all these are cut short here along with Anna Ivanovna's life. Never again will the atmosphere of Christmas in the streets or in the homes be described in the novel. The same is the case with a church funeral. The next funeral described in the novel displays the features which already belong to a different time. At that funeral Lara laments: "All the same, what a pity he isn't having a church funeral. The burial service is so splendid and tremendous!" (p. 446).

Yolka—the term used in the Russian title—can mean fir tree, Christmas tree and also Christmas or New Year's party, when used with the expression 'to be at.' For Yurii Zhivago, Yolka is the symbol of the Christmas festivities, it is the Russian 'adoration of the Magi.' He also identifies it with Blok and his times. Anna Ivanovna's funeral at the end of this chapter also symbolizes the end of an era. This chapter includes a symbol in the title and many other symbols in its text. The title also helps to draw attention to the role of other symbols in this chapter.

Among such symbols is the candle that is lit by Pasha Antipov for Lara and placed on the window-sill. This candle, noticed by Yurii from the street, inspires the following lines: 'A candle on the table burned / A candle burned' (p. 81).

These lines appear afterwards in Yurii's poem 'Winter Night.' Later in the novel, at Yurii Zhivago's funeral, memories connected with this room, that evening and the same candle come to Lara's mind:

> [B]ut she could remember nothing *except the candle burning at the window-sill* and melting a round patch in the icy crust on the glass.
>
> How could she know that *Yurii,* whose dead body was lying on the table, *had seen the candle* as he was driving past, and noticed it, *and from the moment of his seeing its light* ['The candle burned on the table / the candle burned'], *all that was pre-ordained for him had seized control of his life* (p. 446).

The candle in the novel is symbolically connected with the poet. As shown above, it inspires the poet and also symbolizes the poet himself, according to the way Lara addresses him when she finds him writing his poems at night in Varykino:

> "Still at work my love?" she whispered in a voice heavy with sleep. "Burning and shining like a candle in the night." ["And you still are burning and glimmering, my bright little candle!" in Russian original, AM] (p. 393).

Already in the second section of this chapter we find poetical talent is ascribed to Yurii:

> *Yurii thought well and wrote even better.* Ever since his school days he had dreamed of writing a book in prose ... He was too young to write such a book; instead, *he*

wrote poetry (p. 68).

This is the last chapter of the novel in which the events and atmosphere are connected with Blok's time and the celebration of Christmas. The introduction of the candle, noticed by Yurii on his way to the Christmas celebration, and the poetical mood inspired by it symbolically conclude Blok's times and pass the torch to the poet of the next era.

This is confirmed on the last page of the prose text of the novel, where Yurii's closest friends talk about eras and poets and believe that one of the characteristics of a great poet is the talent of foreseeing the future:

> Take that line of Blok's 'We, the children of Russia's terrible years: you can see the difference of periods (epochs) at once.' In his time when he said it, he meant it figuratively, metaphorically. The children were not children but the sons and heirs of the intelligentsia, and the terrors were not terrible but apocalyptic; that's quite different. Now the figurative has become literal, children are children and the terrors are terrible (p. 463).

They say these words when summing up their era, the one that followed Blok's, the times in which they all lived, in which Yurii wrote his poetry.

The reading of Yurii's poetry inspires in them an optimistic outlook toward the future:

> To the two aging friends by the window it seemed that this freedom of the spirit was there, that on that very evening the future had become almost tangible ... *And it seemed that the book in their hands knew what they were feeling and gave them its support and confirmation* (pp. 463-464).

In this chapter the character of the title is pointing toward the symbolic means employed to represent the issues discussed in this chapter.

CHAPTER FOUR:
THE IMMINENT AND THE INEVITABLE

The above title is a literal translation of the Russian. In the English translation the title is 'The Advent of the Inevitable.' The title in translation does not convey the association of the particular events described here as closely as does the Russian title. The word advent may evoke religious associations in English, but in Russian *nazryevshiye* means ripened, mature and, figuratively, imminent.

This chapter describes five years in the life of the major characters. More attention is given to the description of events than of ideas. There is a concise presentation of Lara and Pasha's graduation, their wedding and their departure from Moscow, followed by a short depiction of their life in Yuryatin and the end of family happiness with Pasha's departure for the army as a volunteer. The portrayal of the events in Yurii Zhivago's life during the same period coincides with the appearance of the war in the novel. The details of his personal life during this period (such as his wedding, his graduation, etc.) are left out and so are many details concerning the war (such as the opposing side and when and why the war started). The description of the war begins at a time when the inevitable becomes imminent. The situation is seen from the point of view of Yurii, a Moscow physician, in the second autumn of the war:

> The Moscow hospitals were desperately overcrowded, especially since the battle at Lutsk. The wounded were put in the passages and landings. The general overcrowding was beginning to affect the women's wards (p. 99).

The overcrowding of the hospitals in Moscow after the battle of Lutsk, at a fair distance from Moscow, serves here as a metaphor representing the general situation at the front and the failing logistics of the government to deal with it.

The last four years of Zhivago's life are symbolically summed up by two events: professionally, in a very successful diagnosis for a young doctor, and personally, by the birth of his first child.

The war is the direct cause of Zhivago's separation from his family (he is being drafted) and the indirect cause of the separation of the Antipovs (Pavel volunteers, hoping to solve personal problems), yet both separations are foreshadowed by the title as imminent and inevitable.

In this chapter we find the direct and indirect situations, which Pasternak considers imminent and inevitable, in the lives of the protagonists and in the country. The grotesque case of Gimazetin's wounding represents the horrors of the war. The low morale of the army, the degradation of minorities (in the incident of the Jewish patriarch and the Cossacks), the weak tsar surrounded by strong-willed advisers, the imminent retreat of the army from the front line, the failure to communicate the real situation due to untalented reporters—all represent the disintegration of the country at war. But it is the title that connects these events from different planes of life and emphasizes the critical and common characteristic of the events and facts described here. The author portrays each of the story lines at the moment of imminent change and predicts the nature of these changes through the title. Having presented the common idea of the situation in the title, he proceeds to show us specifically and concretely how it manifests itself in the lives of his characters and the country.

How imminent and inevitable the events described here were is represented symbolically by the timing of the birth of Zhivago's son. (Again the English terms 'giving birth' or 'birth' do not suggest the same association as the old Russian expression used here by the author, *razryesheniye ot bremeni*—release from a [usually heavy] load or burden for the mother). All the other events in the chapter, such as Antipov's volunteering, the mobilization of Zhivago, and the February Revolution, which concludes this chapter, are inevitabilities of the historic time or social nature. The most convincing expression of the common situations, however, is represented by the absolutely indisputable, *imminent and inevitable situation in nature—the timing of the birth of a child*.

The events described here range from a situation in an individual personal life to the social and historical situation in the country, but it is the title that brings them under one and the same roof with the timing of the birth of a child. This is the absolute imminent and inevitable, not given to control by man, the *timing of nature*.

CHAPTER FIVE:
FAREWELL TO THE PAST

In this chapter the title emphasizes those details which are of special importance and could have been understood differently if one were to disregard the title. The fifteenth section of this chapter, presented in the form of an explicit summary, shows a direct connection between the title and the chapter. The preceding sections describe certain details of the new life that followed the February Revolution. The portrayal of the new life is set against the background of the old. By repeated use of words like 'former,' 'now' and 'replaced,' the earlier mode of existence is communicated in a manner that leaves the reader reflecting on the change that has taken place.

At the municipal council in the *new* reality, minor commissars and health department officers are *replaced* by people like Yurii, Lara and Galiulin (p. 147). The hospital in which Zhivago was a patient and now works was housed in a building which in the *former* system belonged to countess Zhabrinskaya: 'Now the house was a hospital, and its owner was under arrest in Petersburg, where she had lived' (p. 151). [Arrested? This seems to belong to the Bolshevik era. AM]

Many things connected to the house are described in their *former* role and their role *now*. Along with the furniture and other things in the house are the Countess's head cook Ustinya and Mademoiselle Fleury, the governess who brought up the Countess's daughters. Their presence in the re-direction of the hospital is presented in a humorous way. Their reaction to the change, through the particular incidents described here, shows a different relation of the Russian and foreign servant to the new reality.

The incident with Gintz relates much more than a single incident of a clash of different strata in the army or in society at large. This incident, unlike most other issues, is given much attention here. Gintz's appearance on the scene of the bleak bureaucratic routine, in the post revolutionary disorganized existence, represents the naive spirit of the February Revolution in contrast to the war reality and the coming spirit of the Bolshevik revolution. Gintz's fragile appearance, his idealistic beliefs and his way of dealing with reality show him out of place and time, but, as we will see later, represent a whole class of people like him, real idealists:

> The centre of the stage was held by the new commissar, the hero of the day and the sensation of the town, who, instead of being at his post, was addressing the rulers of this paper kingdom quite unconnected with staff and operational matters (p. 128).

> The commissar was exactly as he had been described to Yurii: thin and graceful, a boy just out of school room and burning like a candle with the flame of his ideals. He was said to come from a good family ... to have been one of the first to march his company to the Duma in February (pp. 128-129).

Gintz believes that if he will go to the rebels and have a heart to heart talk "they will go back to the positions they have deserted as good as gold."

> "I'll say to them: 'Take my own case. I am an only son, the only hope of my parents, yet I haven't spared myself. I have given up everything—name, family, position ... Did we have to do it? And you, you who are no longer ordinary privates but the warriors of the first revolutionary army in the world ...' " (p. 129).

The needless, brutal murder of Gintz shows the pure-in-heart, highly unselfish ideals in collision with the brute force of blind hatred incited by prejudice and, already then, Bolshevik propaganda. Already in his address to the Meluzeevo crowd Gintz is aware of the undercurrent force of the rebellion:

[H]e spoke with feeling, reproving the people of Meluzeyevo for their disorganized ways and for allowing themselves to be affected by the disintegrating *influence of the Bolsheviks* who, he assured them, were the real instigators of the Zybushkino disorders (p. 132).

Gintz's death, like Anna Ivanovna's funeral earlier, represents yet another facet of the end of an era. It marks the end of a generation of Russian idealists, who sacrificed their lives for the freedom of their country, and who were the first victims of the brutal forces that replaced their idealism.

Along with the new reality in the country appears a new reality in the personal lives of the protagonists. Antipova's name, casually mentioned in Yurii's letter, provokes Tonya's intuitive and correct evaluation of Yurii's feelings for Lara and Lara's role in Yurii's life is foreshadowed.

The situation in the country is conveyed in a very cursory manner: there are now new orders in the administration, new duties for military personnel, new relations between the officers and the soldiers, a new crowd in the Meluzeevo town square, the train stations are overcrowded like never in the past and so forth.

A constant comparison with the old life accompanies the descriptions of the new. Sometimes it is done directly, and sometimes it is understood from the context. Guided by the title one will notice many details which could be missed otherwise or not given their full meaning. Thus Zhivago's departure from Meluzeyevo and his train journey to

Sukhinichi have already all the signs of the new time as facts of the reality *now*. But a remark like 'That night at Sukhinichi, *an obliging, old-style porter* took Yurii over the unlit tracks ...' (p. 145) gets the reader's attention, triggered by the title, and hence widens the text and invokes the comparison of the scenes preceding this encounter with a different reality, one of the past.

In addition to the role the candle plays in the amusing conversation between Yurii and the deaf-mute (when Yurii blows out the candles, the communication between them stops, since Pogorevshikh cannot read Yury's lips in the dark), the symbolic role of the candle ('Yurii's compartment was lit by a guttering candle which stood on a small table ...' [p. 146]) can be seen in the fact that its appearance in the text is soon followed by the section in which Zhivago summarizes in his mind the past and present realities presented in the preceding sections of this chapter. The first candle inspired thoughts about Blok and the Russian celebration of Christmas. This candle inspires thoughts about Russia at this stage of history.

The comparison of the *past* and *present* reality, which until now has been described in life, is summarized in Yurii's thoughts: 'His thoughts swarmed and whirled in the dark. They seemed to move in two main circles, *two skeins* which constantly tangled and untangled themselves' (p. 148).

In the first circle are the thoughts about Tonya, home, the well-arranged former life, a life where the relations between people he remembered were sincere and pure and where also the whole spirit of the times was of similar qualities. For Zhivago, and people like him, the spirit of the times is expressed as follows:

> Here too were his loyalty *to the revolution and his admiration for it,* the revolution in the sense in which it was accepted by the middle classes and in which it had

been understood by the students, *followers of Blok* in 1905.

This familiar circle also contained the foretaste of the new things. In it were *those omens and promises* which before the war, between 1912 and 1914, had appeared in Russian thought, art and life, in the *destiny of Russia* as a whole and in *his own* (p. 148).

In Zhivago's thoughts Blok's Russia belongs to the past. His own destiny and the destiny of Russia are connected, the same way he perceived the relationship of former Russia with Blok. For Zhivago, Blok and the spirit of his Russia belong to the reality of the irrevocable past. (The new Russia will be represented by a new poet. Could it be by him, Zhivago?)

The former (old) reality, to which Zhivago bids farewell in his mind, seems even more irretrievable when seen next to the dynamic, violent new reality of the other circle:

'These new things were not familiar, not led up by the old; they were *unchosen, prescribed by reality* and as sudden and *inevitable* as an earthquake (p. 148).

The new reality for Russia is the war and the bloodshed and the horrors connected with it. The new includes also the revolution, not the one idealized by the students, but the one 'born of the war, bloody, pitiless, elemental—a soldier's revolution, led by its professionals, the *Bolsheviks*' (p. 148). The new reality of Zhivago's personal life includes Antipova. It seems that the character of the *new* described as *unchosen, inevitable and prescribed by reality* for the country characterizes also his personal life and in particular the nature of his relationship with Antipova.

Thus this chapter, which started with scattered sketches of different issues of the new life following the

February Revolution, is monumentally summarized and divided into two circles in Zhivago's thoughts.

The Bolsheviks' role in the general upheaval in the country after the February Revolution is clearly hinted at here, but directly pointed out by Pasternak when he mentions the *church of Christ the Saviour* as Yurii arrives in Moscow: 'Hardly has Yurii noticed it when the church of Christ the Saviour showed over the rim of the hill, and, a moment later, the domes, chimneys ...' (p. 152). (Thus the readers are reminded that the church was demolished by the Bolsheviks by Stalin's orders to make place for the Palace of the Soviets.)

To mention the Church here is the author's farewell to yet another facet of the old Russia and old Moscow.

It is likely that many details would have been missed if not for the title. Thus the above mentioned facts—not by any means all mentioned here—show the structural role of the title.

CHAPTER SIX:
MOSCOW BIVOUAC

The word 'bivouac' is not associated with a stable way of life. Conventionally, it is connected with a temporary, changeable reality. This chapter begins with the arrival of Yurii Zhivago to Moscow and ends with his departure with his family. (The details of their departure are continued in the next chapter.) By using the word 'bivouac' to take the place of the home to which Zhivago mentally was returning from the war, the author hints already in the title at the changed reality Yurii is about to find. As we continue to read through this chapter, we find that there is very little that is permanent in the new life to which he returns. He finds a *change* of circumstances, of people, of relationships. *Change* is the only thing that is constant in this new reality. The new predicament is portrayed in a sketchy manner. The generalized and externalized view of events and situations, shown here, stresses the loss of the individual and private life associated with the idea of home, what Moscow meant for Yurii, and comments on what he found: the bivouac. The change is presented fleetingly and symbolically at different levels of existence:

> [I]t seemed to him when he recalled it later that even then the *crowd* hung about the market only by habit, that already there was no reason for it to be there, because the *stalls were covered up and even locked* and there was nothing to buy or sell in the littered square which nobody swept (p. 153).

This unbelievable rubbish went round the market,

going up in price as it changed hands (p. 153).

These scenes differ from many other descriptions in the novel by generalizing the situation. This kind of approach of presenting the scene from the outside and generalizing phenomena, a method which is not applied elsewhere in the novel, sets the tone for this whole chapter:

> Winter came, just the kind of winter that had been foretold. It was not as terrifying as the two winters that followed it but it was already *of the same sort*: dark, hungry and cold, spent in watching the *destruction of all that was familiar and the changing of all the foundations of life*, and in inhuman efforts to keep hold of life as it slipped out of your grasp (p. 178).

The generalization mode is used even to describe the winter, which is said to belong to the same kind as previous winters: 'These three winters which followed one another have now merged into one and it is difficult to tell them apart' (p. 178).

The lack of elements of personal and private character, usually associated with the meaning of home and not to be found in the bivouac, stresses the impersonal character of relationships here as well as in the dynamics of the plot:

> *The old life and the new ways* [new order, AM] did not yet interlock (p. 178).

> *Everywhere* there were new elections: for the running of housing, trade, industry and municipal services (their composition was changing). *Commissars were being appointed to each* [to all of them, AM], *men in black leather jerkins, with unlimited powers and an iron will, armed with means of intimidation and revolvers, who shaved little and slept*

less (p. 178).

These were the people who reorganized everything in accordance with the plan, and company after company, enterprise after enterprise, became bolshevised (p. 178).

In this chapter there is an absence of the singular, of individual characters, individual voices or opinions. Generalizing everything into two categories of 'old life' and 'young order' (or 'new ways,' as in the English translation), the constant use of words like 'everywhere,' 'to each' ('to all of them'), stereotyping the men of the 'young order,' even by the way they dressed, shaved and slept, is an indirect commentary by the author regarding the people of the new times.

Taking into account that the title, like in the other chapters, has the structural function to highlight certain elements of the content, it is possible to see a parallel when comparing home with bivouac and the 'old life' with the 'young order.' The vanishing of the home is accompanied by the loss of the personal and the private in the new life as shown here. Most of the events described in this chapter acquire an importance of symbolic nature. *The replacing of home with bivouac transfers the centre of attention from personal life, from events relating to individual lives to events of impersonal and general character.* This trend is perpetuated in the summary portrayal of issues belonging to different facets of the new life covering problems concerning the country as a whole and in personal relationships between people:

The people in the towns were as helpless as children in the face of the unknown ... (p. 168).

His *friends had become strangely dim* and colourless. *Not one of them had kept his own outlook, his own world* (p. 160).

In the evening the conversations between *him and Tonya* were of this sort [lost in the English translation, the original text in Russian says: 'In the evening *husband and wife* had conversations of this sort', AM]:

"Don't forget Wednesday, at the Doctor's Union, they will have two sacks of frozen potatoes for us in the basement ... " (p. 179).

The italicized words, on these different levels of existence ('people in the towns,' 'friends,' 'husband and wife'), are all associated with events and phenomena in the plural and are pointing to the loss of the personal, individual. By referring to Tonya and Yurii as *husband and wife*, the talk between them becomes characteristic of the issues of the times. Thus, by referring to them as husband and wife, Pasternak transforms their personal situation to one of general nature.

If one assumes that the home which Zhivago left for the war belonged to the 'old life' then the term bivouac here represents the 'young order' and the new life. The structural role of the title, by foretelling the nature of the change, directs us to look for the data to be found here.

CHAPTER SEVEN:
THE JOURNEY (ON THE ROAD)

With thirty-one sections this is the longest chapter of the novel. Its main theme is Russia at this particular time in its history and it presents a cross-section of its prevailing social problems. The symptoms of the civil war are represented by a wide range of phenomena.

Since antiquity writers have used the road to create situations which are otherwise impossible. Time and space are more easily manipulated on the road than in static conditions. This is how Bakhtin formulates the function of the road in his essay 'Forms of Time and of the Chronotope in the Novel':

> The chronotope of the road associated with encounter is characterized by a broader scope, but by a somewhat lesser degree of emotional and evaluative intensity. Encounters in a novel take place 'on the road.' The road is a particularly good place for random encounters. On the road ('the high road'), the spatial and temporal paths of the most varied people—representatives of all social classes, estates, religions, nationalities, ages—intersect at one spatial and temporal point. People who are normally kept separate by social and spacial distance can accidentally meet; any contrast may crop up, the most various fates may collide and interweave with one another. On the road the spacial and temporal series defining human fates and lives combine with one another in distinctive ways, even as they become more concrete by the collapse of *social distances*.

In the plot of his novel Pasternak utilizes many of the features of the road in literature, as Bakhtin mentions. In this chapter, Pasternak does not dwell on psychological or emotional descriptions of the characters. The kind of people the Zhivagos encounter on the road, the facts and events of the new reality are the main dynamic motifs of this chapter. It is the reasons that brought them on the train, not their individual lives, that are of significance here. The comparatively extensive characterization of Strelnikov is central to the understanding of this chapter. Among other reasons is the need to explore, understand and introduce this new kind of idealistic leader in order to comprehend the men whose acts are ruled by lofty ideals and who, at the same time, are directly responsible for the misery described earlier in the chapter.

The lot of the people described here represents that of people of this generation. *It is not a gallery of types,* but rather *a gallery of fates.* It is not a psychological analysis of human emotions or thought, but a history of human fates. And it is not a typification of people, but a *typification of fates.*

The moving train with its passengers is a micro-cosmos of the country in transition. The interaction of the travellers among themselves and with people at the stations where the train stops presents a cross-section of the general texture of the new reality. With the train moving east into the depth of the country, strata of society and particularities are observed from the *moving train,* such as the three main groups on the train, i.e., the military [translated as 'sailors'], the 'free public' [translated as 'ordinary passengers'], the labour conscripts; the train stations with their individual problems; the new kind of communication between people and institutions; the new class division; the mode of trade; the signs of the civil war; the jargon of the commissars; the means the Bolsheviks use to collect grain; the reason for the burned villages; the incident with the train engineer showing his lack of choice; and many other occurrences of that time. Accordingly, Pasternak describes most of these phenomena in a *fleeting form*. Moving on the train from west to east, along the horizontal axis of Russia, we travel through a series of events and circumstances characteristic of that time. The number and variety of events manifested here may seem implausible to a conventional perception of reality. But when reality no longer fits traditional logic and values, this seems a realistic way to portray it. Yurii's answer to Kostoyed, "But where is reality in Russia today? My belief is that it's been frightened out of existence" (p. 203), relates not only to the situation in Russia but also to the style the author needed to use to describe it.

We do not find authentic dialects here; instead we encounter a form of personal language, mixed with the new jargon of the time. There are also no 'three-dimensional types.' Critics, who found in this chapter the language of the characters not representative of authentic dialects, many scenes unbelievable, and the characters flat, present abundant proof to sustain their argument. Alexander Gladkov's remark that 'All the public scenes, by language, are false: B.L. [Pasternak] does not hear this [the episodes on the train, with the partisans and so on]' (Section 5), or those by other critics accusing Pasternak of presenting flat characters (Sections 6, 7, 8), missed the symbolical dimension of Pasternak's portrayal of life. Pasternak's intention is to *show the reasons* which brought together these different people under a certain category (for instance the labour conscripts, the commissars, the free passengers) and to show how the new order functions. The few stories about several characters (Pritulev, Vassya, Kostoyed) show that the reasons that govern the new grouping of people disregard those characteristics which are traditionally expected to be found in a portrayal of three-dimensional characters. Thus such a depiction of the characters is also Pasternak's indirect comment on what consideration the new system has for the individual and on what strategy it uses to achieve its goals. The stories of Pritulev, Vaska, the incidents—with the train engineer, the snow removal from the tracks, the train refuelling with wood found on the way—all expose the same fact that the individual has no rights in this new life. ('Free' people are ordered to remove snow, to cut wood.) The insignificance of the individual life is stressed by the behaviour of the statistician in Strelnikov's train office, who is concerned with weather statistics, while White and Red Russians kill one another in a fierce battle close by. Thus the author shows that this new life is ruled by numbers rather than a concern with lives.

In this last chapter of the first part of the novel the theme of the free individual—one of the leitmotifs of the novel—is viewed from a different angle. The issues raised in Zhivago's encounter with Strelnikov deal with much more than their different political or personal outlook on life. Actually, there is barely any dialogue between them and in their short encounter there is no discussion about an individual's freedom or rights. Strelnikov appears to Yurii the epitome of perfection, but he is lacking the qualities that, according to the narrator, are absolutely necessary for an individual to be free. And since Pasternak uses a symbolic style, these critical conclusions about Strelnikov are not likely reserved only for him. They may pertain to the theme of the free individual or point to other seemingly 'perfect' leaders of the revolution.

Just before Yurii meets Strelnikov, while watching a young, wounded prisoner of war ramming back his constantly falling school cap on his bandaged head, he reflects:

> There was something symbolical in this absurd action, so contrary to common sense, and, impressed by its significance, Yurii longed to rush out and address the boy in the words which were boiling up inside him. He longed to shout out to him and to the people in the

railway coach *that the salvation lay not in the loyalty to forms and uniforms, but in throwing them away* (p. 224).

As he turns away from the scene, Strelnikov comes into the room. It is clear to Yurii at once that 'this man was a finished product of the will' (p. 224). That he is also 'possessed of a remarkable gift, but it was not necessarily the gift of originality ... might equally be one of imitation' (p. 224). This is followed by a remark that '[i]n those days everyone modelled himself on someone else—imitating the heroes of history ...' (p. 224). The next section, which starts with the question "Who in reality was Strelnikov?" (p. 225), offers enough biographical information to recognize Pasha Antipov in him. We are told that he has only recently escaped from Germany where he was a prisoner of war, and Tiverzin (in whose apartment Pasha Antipov lived as a schoolboy), referred to as 'a railway worker of advanced political views' (p. 225), vouched for him with the ruling authorities. Strelnikov 'justified the confidence of the authorities' (p. 225). His victorious war record, listed in detail, ends with an appraisal, 'In each case he had achieved complete surprise and had investigated, tried, sentenced and enforced his sentences with speed, harshness and resolution' (p. 226).
Strelnikov also had '*an unusual power of logical reasoning, and he was endowed with great moral purity and sense of justice*' (p. 226). It continues:

> But to the task of a scientist breaking new ground, his mind *would have failed to bring an intuition for the incalculable:* the capacity for those unexpected discoveries which shatter the barren harmony of empty foresight.
> And in order to *do good to others he would have needed,* besides the principles that filled his mind, *an unprincipled heart—the kind of heart that knows of no general cases, but only of particular ones, and has the greatness of small actions* (p. 226).

What Strelnikov lacks in his personality and his actions is originality and the moral strength to 'listen to his heart' when it does not agree with the laws and rules of the land. Strelnikov is lacking the qualities which, according to the narrator, are absolutely necessary, if not obligatory, for an individual to be free.

This chapter is the last in the first part of the novel. Although the Zhivagos are still continuing on the train, Pasternak does not conclude the first part with the end of the journey. He chooses to conclude it with Zhivago and Strelnikov's encounter, representing the meeting between 'passive' and 'active' men of history. The author endows the two with such characteristics as idealistic aspirations, moral purity and love for the same woman (it becomes clear at the end of this chapter that Strelnikov is Antipov). Yet we find them on opposite sides of the same historical conflict. The differences between Zhivago and Strelnikov do not originate in their social status as much in the way they view the world and life. In order to stress that the difference between these two men is not based on class dissimilarities, Pasternak, to other objective characteristics that they have in common, adds their pure love for the same woman. Strelnikov's view of the world is stated in this chapter:

> [Strelnikov] has looked upon the world as a vast arena where everyone competed for perfection, keeping scrupulously to the rules. When he found that it was not like that, it did not occur to him that he was wrong in oversimplifying the world order ...
> Embittered by his disillusionment, he was armed by the revolution (pp. 226-227).

While Strelnikov's aspirations to change the world are ruled by principles and ideas, his erroneous perception of life is blamed here on his oversimplifying the world order. Yurii's aspirations are not stated as such here or anywhere else in the novel. We know that he writes poetry, wants to write prose, but it is clear that, more than anything else, he wants to have the freedom to arrive at his own conclusions and follow his own principles. His view of the world is inspired by nature, of which he is constantly aware. (Pasternak uses the context of nature in perception of the world in such characters as Yurii, Lara, Yurii's mother and Nikolay Nikolayevich.) The context of nature is shown to influence Zhivago's thoughts all through the novel. Zhivago symbolizes the 'passive' character in these dynamic times of the revolution. In his thoughts he is concerned with 'the riddles of life, the riddles of death,' believing that life is complex and renewing itself independently of our intervention. Refusing to discuss his views with Strelnikov, Yurii says:

> "But the point you wish me to discuss with you is one I have been arguing with an imaginary accuser all my life, and it would be odd if I had not by now reached some conclusion. Only I could not put it into a couple of words" (p. 228).

Strelnikov's positive qualities, at this stage, mark him as a hero of a Socialist Realism novel. Zhivago's answer to him sounds like Pasternak's comment on the Soviet system. The difference between Strelnikov and Zhivago reaches more widely than the role they play in the plot. Strelnikov, the man of action, in a position of unlimited power over Zhivago (of life and death), insults him by accusing him of sins he has not committed. Strelnikov expresses his suspicions about Zhivago in the rhetoric of the time. Zhivago, on the other hand, while at Strelnikov's mercy, stands up to him and chooses not to respond.

At the end of Book One, this confrontation between Strelnikov and Zhivago can also be seen as a confrontation between the protagonist of a Socialist Realism novel and the protagonist of Pasternak's novel. Taking into account the situation in the country and Pasternak's reaction to it, as can be ascertained from his correspondence at the time he wrote the novel, the dialogue between the two protagonists can be seen as Pasternak's confrontation with the system. When Zhivago says that he has been arguing with an imaginary accuser *all his life,* chronologically this statement may belong more to the author than to his hero. Zhivago is perhaps young for an 'all his life' conclusion.

The title 'On the Road,' has, in this chapter, the classical function of the chronotope of the road: it brings together people of different social strata. The civil war and post-revolutionary Russia are presented through short episodes all connected with the train moving on the railroad. The classical road is replaced by the modern and the random series of episodes described in this chapter reflects the new reality. However, the essence of this reality is presented metaphorically in the dialogue between Strelnikov and Zhivago.

Among other possibilities this can be seen as a dialogue between the 'avenger for world injustice' and the innocent individual victim, between the man ruled by laws and principles of the highest aspirations and the individual ruled by his own conscience and values. *For Strelnikov the end justifies the means; for Zhivago the means of violence can not be justified—the means define the end.* The dialogue between the two, as we know, is continued at the end of Book Two. At this stage in both their lives there are many unknowns in their private lives and in the history of the country. Hope for Strelnikov is at its highest point, while Zhivago's life and existence may at any moment depend at best on people like Strelnikov. The way Zhivago stands up to Strelnikov shows that freedom is not given; it is taken. A free individual is ruled by his conscience. Here it is expressed by Zhivago's courage to defend his position.

In the chronotope of the road, the motion of the train metaphorically extends the geographic space in which the episodes and characters encountered on the train emerge. The intensity of encounters and episodes conveys the relativity aspect of time: the two months (April to June) spent on the road appear much longer to the reader. Because of the symbolic perception of time and space on the road, the incidents described here are not isolated incidents but characteristic of Russian society at that time in history.

PART TWO

CHAPTER EIGHT: ARRIVAL

'Arrival' is the first chapter of the second part of the novel, numbered as the eighth chapter, and is meant to indicate the continuation of the journey. The Zhivagos are still in the same car, but the people highlighted in this chapter of the journey already belong to their new life. The themes and the intonations are focussing on the Zhivagos' reaction to the new reality. The arrival itself is introduced in stages, which are all united by the title. The first stage is felt when they lose their old ties:

> The train which brought the Zhivagos was still standing in the station siding, screened by other trains, but that morning, *for the first time, they felt that their connection with Moscow had snapped and was ended* (p. 231).

This change of feeling is caused by the appearance of a new type of passenger in the Zhivagos' car and at the station:

> All of them, without exception, were acquainted; they waved and called out as soon as they caught sight of each other and they exchanged greetings as they passed. Their speech and dress, their food and manners, were a little different from those of people in the capitals (p. 231).

The impact of the civil war on the peasants is voiced by the sentry accompanying Zhivago to his car:

"The weather has settled down," he was saying, "time to sow the spring corn—oats, millet—it's a golden time for the crops ... Eh, Comrade Doctor, if it wasn't for this civil war and this plague of a counter-revolution, do you think I'd be wasting my time in strange parts at this season? The class war has run between us like a black cat and just look what it does to us" (pp. 231-232).

The meeting between the Zhivagos and Samdevyatov introduces the meaning of *political relativity* in the new reality. Thus, just like the sentry's story speaks for a whole generation of Russian peasants, the evolution of Samdevyatov's political convictions and Mikulitsin and his son's political history represent certain strata of society in pre-revolutionary Russia and their predicament during the changing times.

Samdevyatov points to the highway that runs parallel to the railway:

"That's our famous highway. It runs right across Siberia. The convicts used to sing songs about it. Now it's the operational base of the partisans" (p. 234).

His discussion with Yurii touches upon all kinds of peculiarities and ideological inconsistencies of the time. Yurii's opposition to the new reality can be summarized in two of his utterances:

"Politics means nothing to me. *I don't like people who are indifferent to the truth*" (p. 235).

"I used to be very revolutionary-minded, but now I think that nothing can be gained by violence. *People must be drawn to good by goodness*" (p. 237).

Criticizing Marxism, expressing ideas like the above, to a stranger in front of other strangers, surprises Samdevyatov more than what Yurii is saying, showing indirectly that voicing an opinion which is different from the prevailing one is dangerous. In the conversation between the Zhivagos and Samdevyatov, the latter tells about different people, incidents and other phenomena in the district. They are still on the train and the chronotope of the road still applies to them. Hence, it is not just gossip or stories about isolated episodes but it represents general social problems in Russia of the time in history.

Only after the Zhivagos get off the train (in section 8) and when the train leaves the Torfyanaya station, do their individual feelings and thoughts come into focus again, as if all through the journey the Zhivagos were only on the periphery of action, thus emphasizing the use of the chronotope of the road to survey the country at this particular time.

Once they leave the train, the beauty of nature influences the mood, the thoughts and even the behaviour of the Zhivagos. Individuals, not types like the stationmaster and Bacchus, characters who are out of step with the times, appear on the scene.

The road from the station to Varykino can represent many things, among them the transition from civilization to wilderness, from reality to myth. This change is shown through the appearance and dress of Bacchus, the way he addresses the horses or Tonya and in particular in his language, 'in whose speech archaic idioms, traces of Tartar influence and local oddities of language [were] mixed with those of his own invention' (p. 243).

The creative language and the content of Bacchus's conversation belong to the reality of a fairytale. The beautiful nature surrounding them, images from Anna Ivanovna's stories about the place of her childhood, the character of the driver, install unrealistic hopes in the travellers. But as soon as the roof of the Varykino estate appears on the horizon, rifle shots are heard. They are not fired by the partisans as the Zhivagos thought, but by Mikulitsin, who is trying to scare the wolves. The wolves, in the context of the next visit to Varykino, clearly symbolize danger. Thus, the peaceful journey, the transition from one dangerous reality to another, ends with a warning of new danger.

Again, the Zhivagos' meeting with the Mikulitsins, represented in a lively dialogue between the participants, portrays not only the behaviour of the two families in a rather critical situation, but also refers to the dangers and threats connected with the ideology of the new times.

Even Mikulitsin, who has devoted his life to the liberation movement, is in a situation as he describes:

> "I am caught between two fires—between those who make my life a misery because my son is Red, a Bolshevik, a people's darling, and those who want to know why I was elected to the Constituent Assembly. Nobody is pleased, I have nobody to turn to" (p. 247).

The arrival scene is sealed with the old-world hospitality of the Mikulitsins and with Bacchus muttering, "Mother of God! They've got no more stuff than pilgrims! Nothing but little bundles, not a single trunk" (p. 248).

In the short conversation between the hosts and the guests, past activities come up, showing Liberius's and Antipov's talents. The Zhivagos admire a stereoscope made by Liberius while he was still a child, and Helen is showing off her knowledge in optical physics, taught to her by Antipov, her physics teacher. The association of the lenses and the stereoscope is hardly coincidental. The fact that they relate to the past of the two Communist commanders, described in the novel and turning up in the conversation in the first evening, seems to have a deeper meaning. It could refer to the narrow vision of the two at this time in their lives.

A stereoscope produces a three-dimensional picture; the various lenses produce different images. It might well suggest that, judging from their past, they ought to have turned out less narrow-minded.

CHAPTER NINE: VARYKINO

The preceding chapter gave a systematic description of several stages of the arrival. Like the perspective of a camera set up first at a distance, capturing a less detailed and general view, the focus continuously moves slowly toward Varykino, showing general features characteristic of this chapter of the country and closing in on the house and its inhabitants in Varykino. From a wide view and from a distance, it moves to a close-up, from generalizations to the particular. Stylistically, it proceeds from Samdevyatov's stories about the hosts to the hosts telling about themselves. On the last page of the preceding chapter, in the middle of the tumult of survival issues, the focus is accidentally tilted and captures a stereoscope built by Liberius, Mikulitsin's son, followed by the startling, incongruous questions of the hostess:

"And now this is what I would like to know. How many kinds of lenses are there, *and when are the images real, reversed, natural or inverted?*" (p. 250).

It is no accident that this question, amusing due to the circumstances in which it is asked, concludes the chapter about the arrival. It can, as mentioned in the comments on the former chapter, refer to the two Bolshevik commanders, but considering the content of this chapter, it may have an additional meaning. Due to the method used in the description of the arrival, and due to the fact that this chapter starts with Yurii's diary, the positioning of this question at the end of the previous chapter points in two directions. The first is aimed to lay bare the method used in the portrayal of the new reality in the preceding chapter, and the second points to Yurii's diary with which this chapter opens. Enclosing the diary text in quotation marks alerts the reader to the fact that Yurii's diary is a reflection of life and as such depends on the 'lens' through which it is seen. Zhivago's diary is a document about thoughts of life's events and as such is a *reflection of life,* a reality one stage removed from the primary event of life and transformed by Zhivago's vision. Through which lenses is the reality transformed in Yurii's notes? At what is the focus aimed? What happens in Varykino plays a central role in the plot and the story of the novel. Yurii's diary and the events that follow during Yurii's first stay in Varykino after he stops writing the diary gather all the central themes of the novel. The joy of labouring for the needs of one's family, planting a garden in the spring, collecting the harvest in the fall, reading with friends and family in a warmly lighted room during the long winter evenings are central themes as are the dreams and hopes of the expectant mother, religion and art, love and politics, life and literature. Some themes are allotted more space than others, but the list of the topics included in this chapter makes it look like a shorthand report of many central issues of the novel.

The title of this chapter, 'Varykino,' is not directing the reading as we have seen in other chapters until we look at it as the place where Zhivago writes. Then the meaning of the title assumes a structural role. During Zhivago's first stay he writes his diary; during the second stay, he writes his poems. This time he writes about his thoughts on art in general and about major Russian writers. The next time he writes poems himself and shows how art is born. Thus, Varykino is meant to be for Zhivago what Peredelkino is for Pasternak and Mikhailovskoye for Pushkin—the place where they write their major works. Like on the other topics he touches, in Zhivago's diary we find only short remarks regarding Russian writers and poets, e.g., Pushkin, Chekhov, Nekrasov, Gogol, Dostoyevsky and Tolstoy, as follows:

> What I have come to like best in Russian literature is the childlike Russian quality of Pushkin and Chekhov, their shy unconcern with such high-sounding matters about the ultimate purpose of mankind or their own salvation ... these two were destructed, right up to the end of their lives, by the current, individual tasks imposed on them by their vocation as writers (p. 259).

Remarks like the above single out the few Russian men of letters who avoided preaching. More space, compared to other matters, is given to the examination of the nature of art. Yet the reasons that prevent Zhivago from practising medicine or writing converge in the following:

> What is it that prevents me from being useful as a doctor or writer? I think it is not so much our privations or our wandering or our constantly changing and unsettled lives, as the *power in our day of rhetoric, of the cliché—all this 'dawn of the future,' 'building a new world,' 'torch-bearers of mankind'* (p. 258).

For Zhivago, the creative person, the potential poet, all the problems of his time symbolically converge in the 'word,' and he sees the word's loss of its meaning in the rhetoric of the day as a major tragedy of the time.

Life for Zhivago is interwoven with art, hence the constant shifting from one to the other in his thoughts. In this chapter, Zhivago's thoughts about art, presented in 'written form,' precede his 'vocally' expressed opinion about life later when he meets Lara. Zhivago the individual emerges in his comment on the prevailing slogans of the time:

> "For them, transitional periods, worlds in the making, are an end in themselves. They aren't trained for anything else ... *Man is born to live, not prepare for life.* Life

55

itself—the gift of life—is such a breath-taking serious thing!" (p. 269).

What Zhivago values in the individual lies in his differing from the general, preconceived norm:

"It's good when a man is different from your image of him. *It shows he is not a type* ... But if you can't place him in a category, it means that *at least part of him is what a human being ought to be. He has a grain of immortality*" (p. 268).

About the division of people into isolated entities he agrees with Lara that:

It's only in bad novels that people are divided into two camps and have nothing to do with each other. In real life everything gets mixed up! (p. 270).

The continuously reappearing sign of 'Moreau & Vetchinkin. Sowing Machines, Threshing Machines' is, symbolically, a comment on empty words representing empty deeds. Earlier in his diary Yurii describes the spring sowing and then harvesting in the fall. The joy which comes with such a normal sequence of events in agricultural life represents the 'just sequence' of events in life in general. 'One must reap as one has sown' is also a Russian proverb connecting figuratively the just sequence of events as dictated by nature: in order to harvest one has to sow first. The metaphoric role of the sign is reinforced when considering the context in which the sign reappears. For the first time it appears during Samdevyatov's introduction to Yurii of this part of Russia: 'There were red oil tanks on the skyline, and large advertisements on wooden hoardings. One of them caught Yurii's eye...' (p. 235), along with the signs, facts, mentioned by Samdevyatov, only symbolically represented, from the social, commercial and industrial life of the district. Those elements that were part of the former life vanished, and as witnesses to their former existence are the signs which still remain as part of the contemporary landscape. If to compare what life offered before and the life as shown now, it is possible to see in the sign a silent reminder of a former life, where the sequence of the two functions—sowing and threshing—is representative of the cycle of normal agricultural life. Today, as we have seen from the thoughts of the sentry in the beginning of the preceding chapter, the peasants are not sowing. And while there can be no positive result from threshing without sowing, it seems that by the rhetoric noise and strategy of the new regime, all that is going on is threshing. Thus the role of the sign is to render a picture of the past that has now been distorted.

As will be shown later, there is an ongoing commentary by the author in reference to the system on different levels of existence. Here, through the sign, Pasternak continues his comments on the topic of industrialization and commerce and shows that the industrialization of Russia did not start with the October Revolution as often claimed. This is substantiated by the advertising signs seen from the train when entering the suburbs of the fictitious town of Yuryatin. The advertising signs seen from the train are a reminder of a dynamic commercial life and industrial development that existed there before. The fate of the reappearing sign that symbolizes them all and is discussed with Samdevyatov explains the fate of the institutions represented by the signs. Like in the case of 'Moreau & Vetchinkin,' previously a successful business, they do not operate anymore. Until this point in the story, the sign appeared when the Zhivagos were entering the area of their destination, also when Zhivago looked from Lara's window at his first visit to her apartment and, again, when Zhivago was taken by the partisans.

It seems that the main role of the sign is to bring in the past at dynamic moments of the present, at moments when the future like the past becomes an integral part of the present. That the full meaning of the present is realized when remembering the past and foreseeing the future is a position stressed in Pasternak's philosophy of life as expressed in other passages of his writings.

The notion that this chapter is like a shorthand report of the major themes discussed in the novel is also supported by the repetition of themes that have been discussed earlier in different contexts. The role of the mother in pregnancy (in the diary) is complementing the earlier extended portrayal of giving birth (chapter four). The predicament of the Jewish population, to represent any isolated minority not protected by the laws of the land, previously shown in context of the war with a foreign power (chapter four), is repeated here in the circumstances of the Civil War. In both cases, the attitude of the Jews toward Christ, which paraphrases the motif of a prophet not being recognized in his own town, seems also to be a general accusation of those who stick blindly with tradition. And in the relatively extended (as compared to other themes) discussion about art, we find a different angle of the same issue: 'The fabulous is never anything but the commonplace touched by the hands of genius' (p. 259), when speaking about Pushkin in this chapter, compared with 'because facts don't exist until man puts into them something of his own, some measure of his own wilful, human genius— of fairy tale, of myth' (p. 116). The characters of Strelnikov, Lara, Tonya and Samdevyatov are all seen through Yurii's eyes.

Zhivago's opinions on the independence and creative talents of life itself are confirmed in practice in the last section of this chapter. The love between Yurii and Lara proves to be stronger than the principles that rule their lives. As if to confirm Yurii's theories, this time (through facts) the same statement is made by life itself. The outside forces of life, interfering with the individual's plans, are shown again when Yurii and Lara's decision to follow their principles and to straighten out things between them and Tonya is thwarted by another twist of life when Yurii is forced to join the partisans the very day this decision is made.

Doctor Zhivago, like other works by Pasternak, exhibits the special intricacy of style that is created with links left out between the idea and the facts through which he chooses to present his text. To trace the path to the main idea, which unites all the fragmentary descriptions, discussions and visions, is not always easy. It seems that the relationship between life and art, which captivated Pasternak's interest throughout his life and may be one of the main ideas uniting all his work, is presented here on different levels. While Moscow is a real city, Yuryatin and Varykino are fictitious and as such represent different realities. That they are meant to be generic names (inspired by real places) can be confirmed by the following quote from a passage published in 1938 in Pasternak's *Uyezd at the Home Front*: 'It [Yuryatin] already was representing nothing, was only reflecting, like in a mirror, the changes taking place in the country and at the front line'.

Thus when we read of the Zhivagos cutting off their connection with Moscow and entering the new world, we understand that it refers to more than geographical changes. It means a transformation from reality to myth. Part of 'Arrival' and this chapter move the centre of gravity from life to art. When Samdevyatov leaves the train, Tonya says, "I feel he has been sent to us by fate. I think he will play some helpful part in our lives" (p. 240). And a while later, the station manager says, "Who doesn't know Anfim Yefimovich, the wonder worker! He's our only hope—our one prop ..." (p. 242).

The reaction of the station manager is in vocabulary closer to myth (even more so in Russian: *volshebnik* means 'wizard' instead of 'wonder worker' and *kormilets* instead of 'our one prop' signifies 'provider' in a wide range of meanings). "We have a sort of flying carpet. A friend of ours ..." (p. 250). In Russian fairytales *skatert'—samobranka* is a tablecloth that can magically cover itself with all kinds of food.

This is how Helen, Mikulitsin's wife, refers to Samdevyatov. And when Yurii first hears his name, he thinks: "With a name like that, he ought to have come straight out of an old Russian ballad, complete with a bushy beard, a smock and a studded belt" (p. 232).

Bacchus is another character who may more easily be associated with a fairytale than contemporary life. His appearance, language, song and behaviour (the way he addresses the horses and Tonya), display an aspect of myth, including his observation about the Zhivagos' luggage, which he compares to that of pilgrims. Mikulitsin first responds to the arrival of the Zhivagos with despair and verbal aggression, fitting the political situation in the land, then tunes in to fate and expresses his myth-inspired invitation in church Slavonic: "Anyhow, we aren't Janissaries, we aren't heathens, we won't drive you out into the forest to be eaten by bears" (p. 248).

The mythical aspect of life is continued when Yurii's diary ends with the following observation:

> Perhaps in every life there has to be, besides the other characters involved in it, a secret, unknown force, a figure who is almost symbolical and who comes unsummoned to rescue, and perhaps in mine Yevgraf, my brother, plays a part of this hidden spring of life (p. 261).

It is conspicuous that throughout the tragic and farcical situation of their arrival to Varykino, what Yurii notices, with amazement, is Mikulitsyn's study: "What a wonderful place you have! What a splendid study, it must be a perfect place to work in, a real inspiration!" (p. 250).

Yurii will write his poems in this study, at the very desk he admired, at his next stay in Varykino. Paying attention to it in the predicament they were in that evening shows that Yurii's writing is associated with Varykino. This is substantiated a page later when Yurii's diary opens the ninth chapter. As mentioned earlier, the first nine sections of the chapter which is his diary concern issues regarding art. He concludes his diary expressing the belief that life has its own pattern that is beyond our reasoning. This suggestion plays out on the empirical level of life in the sections that follow and until the end of the novel. The connection between the beliefs and the practical proofs, however, is never shown directly and leaves room for various different readings of the text.

CHAPTER TEN: THE HIGHWAY

In several of the preceding chapters (five, eight and nine) the many changes in the country are observed from a moving train. They have been presented fleetingly (as seen from a train in motion) and each of the events encountered represents a condition prevailing in the country at the time. The changes which have occurred because of the war, the two revolutions and the Civil War are shown, in most cases, through a variety of episodes involving individual lives. Thus, the new political situation in the country, affecting large numbers of people, is presented through the effects it has on particular individuals. The train is a device to bring together representatives from a wide spectrum of society. From the train on which Yurii travels from Meluzeevo to Moscow the issues brought to the reader's attention are mostly results of the war: the war has uprooted many people; the war's harsh reality has changed their values beyond the point of return. The short-lived government of Kerensky, built on values of a pre-war reality, has been unable to establish order in the chaos created by the war. The new people in the municipalities, the overcrowded train stations run by new inexperienced staff, Gintz's tragic encounter with the disobedient army fleetingly represents but a few of the problems with which the new order has had to struggle. The new political reality is feeding on the chaos created by the war and Bolshevik ideology. As Yurii Zhivago reflects "... this new upheaval, today's born of the war, bloody, pitiless, elemental, the soldier's revolution, organized by the experts of these elements, the bolsheviks" (p. 148). During this short journey Yurii reflects on the changes in people's values. The

63

only conversation on this train journey is between Yurii and the deaf-mute revolutionary, who reminds him of Peten'ka Verkhovensky (Dostoevsky's hero from *The Possessed* who is the symbol for power politics of chaos as an end in itself). Panfil Palykh, on the city council (as we find out later), and this deaf-mute revolutionary do not support the ideology of the temporary government. The professional revolutionaries foreshadow the experts of this chaos. A year later, looking at the country from the train on which the Zhivagos travel from Moscow to Yuryatin, the events encountered inside and outside the train are already governed by the Bolsheviks. The train goes through a part of the country under Bolshevik rule. The war has not reached this part of the country. Signs of the Bolshevik victory are already evident everywhere. The burned-down villages seen from the train show the cruelties of the Civil War that still continues. The new stratification of society is at the centre of this journey, but observations are restricted only to events and locations visible from the train. About the situation of the peasants in the villages that are not seen from the train one can only speculate, as does Yurii in his discussion with Kostoyed (p. 202).

Chapter ten, 'The Highway,' one of the shorter chapters consisting of only seven sections, is the only chapter of the novel where the major characters are absent. The present political situation is described sparingly while the past is given a rather dominant representation. Both are presented in the form of a stream of consciousness of Galuzina, the wife of a local grocer. Since her own family 'were simple people who came of peasant and worker stock' (p. 280), she speaks for the largest class of old Russia's population. Her family's achievements tell about the possibilities that were open to the hard-working peasants and workers in Russia before the revolution. In her mind, the war changed the values of the people and the civil war has little to do with justice or betterment of life. Considering when the novel was written, it is not surprising that these issues are discussed in the only chapter of the novel where the White Army in power is described. We encounter here the insider's view of the small towns and villages, representing old Russia. They are visible from the old highway and cannot be seen from the train. The life of these villages is connected with the functions and location of the highway:

> It was the ancient mail road, the oldest highway in Siberia. *It cut through the towns like a knife, slicing them in half like a loaf of bread along the line of their main streets* ... In the distant past, before the railway came to Khodatskoye, the mail was rushed along the highway by troikas ... Those who lived along the highway were like one family. Friendship and marriage linked village to village and town to town (p. 277).

As we learn in this chapter, the Civil War, like the highway, cut like a knife even into the families. The rich past of the highway included the mail troikas, 'caravans of tea, bread and pig-iron, travelled one way (west) and convicts under guard on foot were driven the other (east). Khodatskoye stood on the crossing of the highway and the railway' (p. 277). The meeting of the highway and railway stands for the evolutionary development of events in the past. Such developments were ruled by natural demands of life, by evolution. When the railway reached a town, it contributed to the development of mechanical shops to serve the railway.

'Free' exiles, political prisoners, who served their term and had the required qualifications, were allowed to settle and work as mechanics. Life was ruled not by ideologies and decrees imposed from above, but rather by practical considerations.

The area was so independent that for some time it even had its own Siberian Provisional Government. But the revolution changed its independent way of life. Now it was under the rule of Admiral Kolchak, Supreme Commander of the Whites, engaged in defending the area against the Reds.

Like elsewhere in the novel, Pasternak shows old Russia and its social classes through lists of names of people, locations and even occupations. Such lists become even more significant considering the new names which came to Russia with the October Revolution. In this chapter, the names of villages and small towns—left out of the English translation—show the different way of naming and the variety of settlements that existed before the October Revolution in Russia. 'Stanitsa' is a Cossack settlement; "pochinok,' a forest clearing, or a small new settlement; 'zaimka,' like the former, with a variation in land ownership; 'sloboda,' a settlement exempted from normal state obligations; 'stanok,' a postal station (where horses could be changed) or a small settlement in Siberia; 'selo,' a village. The nomenclature of these locations renders an additional variety of descriptions that all point to a functional settling of the land and, accordingly, a history in naming places different from the one employed by the Soviet institutions, in which many names were derived from communist ideology, often in combination with the colour red. Others were various derivatives of the names of heroes of the revolution. The cultural side of the ideological change of the landscape is even more pronounced by such a landmark as the Monastery of the Exaltation of the Cross and a town named Krestovozdvizhensk (literally, town of the Exaltation of the Cross). The names of places listed here that originate in an evolutionary development of life invite a comparison with the monolithic Soviet era in which Red Star, Red Commune and other combinations of red with Soviet symbols replacing these names. Thus, the poet in Pasternak suffers that the 'word' is insulted and thwarted by the system. Here he shows the shift in political reality through the change in names. Occasionally, by introducing various names that existed before the revolution, without speaking about the changes that took place (except for the Moscow hospital in which Yurii worked, Hospital of the Holy Cross, now known as the Second Reformed Hospital (p. 178), Pasternak is raising major issues about Soviet cultural policy. Throughout the novel, parallel to the changes taking place in the life and values of the country, attention is paid to the changes taking place in the language. Here the linguistic changes are shown by listing the names of places, people, professions and different dialects of old Russia, facts of a past unknown to a new generation of Soviet readers.

Following the bends and twists of the road, the importance of the 'point of view' is highlighted:

> At one stage of the journey the road kept climbing uphill, *giving an ever wider view over the country*. It seemed as if there would be no end to the slow ascent or the *widening of the horizon ... they found that they reached the summit of the hill* (p. 277).

The view opened to the traveller reveals the monastery and the town that are named after the Exaltation of the Cross. In tune with the symbols of the location the time of the year is given as: 'It was the holy week, the end of Lent' (p. 278).

Another peculiar point of view is that of little boys who climbed the belfry to whom the houses down below looked like little white boxes jumbled close together:

> *Little black people, hardly bigger than dots,* walked among the houses .... They stopped to read the decree calling up three more age groups; its text has been posted up on the walls by order of Admiral Kolchak (p. 278).

Most of the information regarding the place and some of the events playing out here are presented from Galuzina's point of view:

> 'The war has killed off the flower of Russia's manhood ... before the war Russia too (like she) had been a marriageable girl in those days, courted by real men, ... now nothing but civilian left ...' (p. 280).

It is not clear whether Galuzina's stream of consciousness is triggered by her lonely walk through the centre of town, or, vice versa, her thoughts make her walk there. Walking through the streets, she remembers the life in these streets before the war. Repeating six times when referring to the locations as 'there' and 'here,' Galuzina turns over in her mind various people from the past who represented different groups of the social spectrum of the town's population. The last group she thinks about consists of the exiled revolutionaries, Tiverzin, Antipov and 'Black Banner' Vdovichenko, the local locksmith. She sees them as people who:

> ... had spent their lives dealing with machines and they were cold and merciless as machines themselves ... they smoked through bone cigarette-holders and they drank boiled water for fear of catching something ... these men would turn everything upside-down, they would always get their way (p. 283).

These observations are made, according to Galuzina's own judgment, by a 'simple woman with a mind of her own, intelligent and young for her age' (p. 283). In the last two sections of this chapter we can easily find confirmation for many of her observations. Thus, Galuzina, the passive observer, may represent the passive people of Russia, who, like she, were unable to practice their beliefs.

The last two sections of this chapter show the Red and White leadership, the people responsible for the changes that decide the fate of people like Galuzina and her family. A secret meeting is described of the Reds in the territory of the Whites. After just hearing about him in Varykino, the first appearance in person in Galuzina's backyard is of Liberius, the Red partisan leader, joined by other commanding officers of the Red leadership. Their behaviour seems to confirm some of her ideas regarding Tiverzin and Antipov as do the speeches at the farewell party for new recruits conscripted by Kolchak. The concluding events of this chapter leave the impression that the changes which befall this region and the rest of Russia were not planned or designed by 'great' people. They were the result of misunderstandings and underestimating the power of empty words. The various linguistic renderings of ideologies, the appreciation of different linguistic talents (Kostoyed is impressed by Liberius's talent to express himself as are Terentii's friends by that of Terentii's father's talent), the vocabulary specific to the Reds (chapter six) and to the Whites (chapter seven), explanation of the meaning of *'sabotazh'*—all this points to the importance of the power of the 'word' and the inherent danger in the empty word.

CHAPTER ELEVEN: FOREST BROTHERHOOD

The title of this chapter in Russian is 'Forest Warriors' and it brings to mind folk legends about old warriors, about those strongmen who fought for the freedom and well-being of their nation. However, in the opening paragraph of the chapter, we are cautioned to differentiate between appearance and reality, which can also apply to the title and the text:

'It looked as if Yurii's captivity, his dependence, were an illusion, as so he were free ... But although he was not fettered, chained or watched, Yurii had to submit to his unfreedom, imaginary though it appeared' (p. 298).

Later we read about the two fighting armies, the Reds and the Whites, along the highway or parallel to it: 'The villages and small towns along the way were Red or White according to the fortunes of war. *It was difficult to tell by looking at them in whose power they lay at any particular moment*' (p. 298).

The activities of the Reds described in this chapter, like the incident with the pharmacy, dealings with war loot, the raid of the village of Veretenniki as a reprisal for withholding food supplies, and other characteristic behaviour of the warriors, which is eclipsed by their leader Liberius's cocaine addiction, are not manifestations of the strength or courage of legendary warriors. Calling the Reds 'warriors' becomes even more oxymoronic when the enemy they are fighting is represented by a unit of idealistic young cadets armed with unnecessary bravery:

Their response to duty, as they understood it, filled them with an ecstatic bravery, unnecessary and provocative ... they walked defiantly upright, neither running nor throwing themselves on the ground, although the terrain was irregular enough to give them cover. *The bullets of the partisans mowed them down* (p. 301).

Again, unnecessary bravery with needless losses of life is not a motif of old heroic legends. The different versions of the same text of the ninetieth psalm, which are found in the amulets of the two soldiers, one fighting for the Reds and the other for the Whites, show how with time a sacred text can be misquoted (changed beyond recognition) with popular use, and also that the two fighting sides belong to different classes of the same culture. Does Pasternak hint here about what happened to the ideals of the revolution in popular use or implementation? The tragedy of war, civil war, culminating in *Soviet political purges* many years later, are summed up in the following lines:

'The text was believed to be miraculous and a protection against bullets. It was worn as a talisman by soldiers in the last imperialist war. *Decades later prisoners were to sew it into their clothes and mutter its words in jail when they were summoned at night for interrogation*' (p. 303).

Theory and practice are shown as being divergent when the indoctrination of the soldiers, the spiritual food, is given more attention than are their daily needs (p. 305). The selfish leader of the partisans is a cocaine addict and preaches what he himself does not practice. Yurii's thoughts about him: 'Just like a gramophone record ... He can't stop. Why isn't he ashamed to chew the same cud all these years?' (p. 307), sum up one side of Liberius. His other side shows him ruthless enough to kill his comrade in arms, Vdovichenko, for fear of losing his position of leader to Vdovichenko. With the character of Liberius Pasternak foreshadows Stalin and many other Soviet leaders. We learn here of a psychic illness, 'which is typical of our time and is directly caused by the historical circumstances' (p. 309), as well as the sentencing of vodka distillers.

It is here that Yurii is summing up his relationship with Liberius and feels open hatred toward him. Observing a butterfly camouflaged in its environment, his mind turns to:

[W]ill and purpose as superior forms of adaptation; mimicry as protective colouring; the survival of the fittest and whether natural selection is indeed the way of the development and birth of *consciousness* (p. 312).

His reflections led him from Darwin to Schelling, from the butterfly to modern painting and impressionist art. He thought of *creation, creatures, creativeness, craft and cunning* (p. 312).

What a combination of concepts this is in the most dangerous place Yurii ever found himself (overhearing a conspiracy meeting to kill Liberius)! How impressionistic, symbolic and provocative is this combination? Consciousness and creation. Could mimicry and pretension be vying here with consciousness for their place in creation?

CHAPTER TWELVE:
ICED ROWANBERRIES

In this chapter, like in the preceding one, the Forest Brotherhood and Doctor Zhivago's captivity are described. We find here a concentration of more cruel, brutal scenes than in any other chapter of the novel. The execution of the conspirators, of distillers, the horrors connected with the women and children joining the soldiers, and finally the arrival of the bleeding stump of a man, victim of the Whites with his message about their atrocities, leading to Panfil's slaughter of his own family—all this completes the list of atrocities described in this chapter.

The descriptions of the place where the executions took place, as a reminder of the heathen times, the behaviour of the executed and their former brothers in arms as executioners, Vdovichenko's behaviour and his last words can all be seen as a continued critique of the new Bolshevik leaders and the end of dedicated idealists:

> "Don't humble yourself! Your protest will not reach them. These new 'oprichniki,' these master craftsmen of new torture chambers will never understand you! But don't lose heart. History will tell the truth. Posterity will nail the Bourbons of the comissarocracy to a pillar of shame, it will pillory their dark deeds. We die as martyrs at the dawn of the world revolution. Hail, revolution of the spirit! Hail, universal anarchy!" (p. 321?).

Then there is the title of this chapter. On one hand the Russian title—rowan berries with sugar—could be a Russian dessert. And do not the above listed cruelties seem to be a full meal, more than enough for the doctor? What is the presumed dessert here about?

On the other hand, the rowan tree itself becomes a kind of leitmotif of this chapter. Considering the associations it brings to Zhivago's mind, its role in the chapter is parallel to the role of Lara in his life. It becomes even more convincing when attention turns to the concluding section of this chapter, in which the meeting between Yurii and the rowan tree takes place:

> It was covered half in snow, half in frozen leaves and berries and it held out two white branches welcomingly. He remembered Lara's strong white arms and seized the branches and pulled them to him. As if in answer, the tree shook snow all over him. He muttered senselessly; "I'll find you, my beauty, my love, my rowan tree, my own flesh and blood" (p. 338).

From its first appearance, the rowan is not just a beautiful tree, but an animated tree. The role of the rowan tree in the song of Kubarikha acquires legendary dimensions in the metamorphosis of the hare into the soldier in a foreign land, the rowan tree into Zhivago's beloved. If we pay attention to the analysis of the Russian song, these last lines show even more clearly the role the rowan tree plays in Zhivago's decisions:

> By every possible means—by repetition and similes—it [the song] attempts to stop or to slow down the gradual *unfolding of a theme*, until it reaches the mysterious point, then it *suddenly reveals itself* (p. 327).
>
> We find in the end of Kubarikha's song: "Homesick, I—poor soldier, kept in foreign parts / I will escape out of my bitter durance, / I will go to my red berry, my fair love" (p. 327).

At the end of the song, we find a hint to the soldier's intention to run away from his captivity, to his 'red berry' his 'fair love' which, according to the above analysis of the Russian song, is its main meaning. As we see later, Kubarikha's song left an imprint on Zhivago's mind, since next time when he listens to Kubarikha casting a spell, his thoughts turn to Lara again.

> Yurii was sufficiently well read to realize that Kubarikha's last words have been the opening passage of an ancient chronicle ... Why then should the nonsensical images thus handed down have gripped and moved him with the force of real events?
>
> Lara's left shoulder was open. Like a key turning in the lock of a secret safe ...
>
> How well he loved her, and how lovely she was, in exactly the way he had always thought and dreamed and needed. Yet what was it that made her so lovely? Was it something that could be named or singled out in a list of qualities? A thousand times no! She was lovely by virtue of the matchlessly simple and swift line which the creator at a single stroke had drawn around her [from top to bottom, AM] in this divine outline she has been handed over, like a child tightly wound up in a sheet after its bath, into the keeping of his soul (p. 331).

The content of this chapter and the role ascribed to the rowan tree in the forest, and the conclusion of Kubarikha's song, show that his longing for Lara is the force that gives Yurii the impulse to run away from his captivity. And since getting to pick berries from the rowan tree is the excuse Yurii gives to the sentry when escaping, it again shows that the title is pointing to the essence of the contents of the chapters. Here, the rowan tree, a metaphor for the beloved, inspires both the soldier in the Russian song and Yurii to run from their captivity.

The meaning of the Russian title in English is 'Rowan Tree Berries in Sugar.' 'Riabina' in Russian can mean both the tree and the berries. Frozen rowan berries with sugar, in some parts of Russia, is a dessert. When one looks at the content of this chapter in view of the above, one can enter into Zhivago's mood when he makes up his mind to escape—he has just had enough, enough of cruelty, injustice and horrible suffering of the people in the forest. And the senseless propaganda of Liberius is the last straw, the last course of his 'heavy meal.' He opts for life, he opts for its force, he walks toward the rowan tree, a metamorphosis of Lara in his thoughts.

It is in the forest, located in Siberia, that we find open confrontation with the Soviet regime. It is not obvious at first glance, since in the beginning the Forest Brotherhood looks like an isolated episode of the Civil War. It seems that also the problems and issues are limited to this particular place and this group of people. But when we put together the two chapters in the forest, we soon see that we are dealing with a micro-cosmos of problems and issues that apply to the Soviet regime at the time described and also later.

It is interesting that Pasternak chose the forest in Siberia. In the chapter preceding the Forest Brotherhood we have been given a good sense of what life was like in Siberia before the revolution. Galuzina's walk around town and her thoughts about the past way of life draw for us an image of a past very different from what the Soviet regime claims it to be. It shows a well-functioning society, both in town and in the countryside. Even when running to the forest the women bring with them a great many cows. The cows are mostly of a Swiss breed of black and white markings (Holsteins, perhaps), highly profitable dairy cattle of foreign origin, which at the time the novel was written did not exist in Russia.

'The cows were almost all black and white and belonged to some Swiss breed popular in Siberia' (p. 328).

In many places, in subtle hints, Pasternak tries to restore a truthful picture of the past, without which the Soviet state cannot be evaluated correctly. Different levels of existence in the past are symbolically presented throughout the novel. Changing the facts about the past (as in Orwell's *1984*) seems to be necessary for a totalitarian regime. Pasternak understood this and therefore showing the reader the truth of the past was an important part of the message the novel set out to deliver. The past was so misrepresented that in 1955 and 1956 even the censors did not react adversely to the revelations of truth which were dispersed throughout the novel.

Pasternak has a special role for Kubarikha. Nobody takes her seriously, she speaks such nonsense that one can easily refrain from attaching any significance to her. She plays a role of a veterinarian, of a psychotherapist, improviser of a folk song and an old chronicle; she is Zhivago's 'competitor' in his profession as a physician and as a writer. It is also she who questions the reality or meaning of the red banner as a flag, and it is she who substitutes the endorsed slogan of the revolution 'Proletarians of the World Unite' with 'Come to Me, All Ye Poor and Proletarians of the World.'

Thus the two chapters in the forest are full of critical remarks about the revolution and the Soviet state. Some of them are open; others, concealed. Many of them are found with the guidance of the titles.

CHAPTER THIRTEEN: OPPOSITE THE HOUSE OF CARYATIDS

The name of this house and its role in the life of the city have been described already in the ninth chapter of the novel:

> The 'House of Caryatids' was a dark, steel-grey building with statues of the Muses holding cymbals, lyres and masks decorating its façade. *A merchant* [theatre-lover] *has built it in the last century as his private theater.* The merchant's heirs had sold it to the Merchant Guild, which gave its name to the street, and the whole district was known by the name of the house [with caryatids]. *It was now used by the Party's Town Committee* and the lower part of its façade, *where posters and programs had hung in the old days, now displayed government proclamations and decrees* (p. 265).

In a rough comparison, one can say about the history of this house the same as what Gordon says about the Russian Revolution: "This has happened several times in history. A thing which has been conceived in a lofty, ideal manner becomes coarse and material. Thus Rome came out of Greece and the Russian Revolution came out of the Russian enlightenment" (p. 463).

But, the lion's share what is described in this chapter takes place *opposite* the House of Caryatids, and many comparisons between these two houses are solicited by the title of the chapter. The role of the theatre and the Party's Town Committee are compared here and seen as opposing one another. There is nothing said about what might have been the content of the posters and programs of the theatre, but, on the other hand, the content of government proclamations and decrees are quoted at length. The posters and programs of the theatre are ascribed to bygone days, and the proclamations and decrees to the present. Quoting the content of the decrees in the language of the present, and not mentioning the possible content of posters and programs of the past, is a tacit statement that the language of the old days does not exist anymore. The new vocabulary of the decrees contains words and expressions like: 'labour books,' the 'hoarding of food,' 'not belonging to the exploiting class,' 'will be prosecuted with the utmost rigor under the wartime regulations' (p. 339). The language of the decrees and the new nomenclature show the new values of the present time.

The House of Caryatids was first a theatre. The exterior of the house corresponded to its first designation. Now it is occupied by the Party's Town Committee. With its present designation, the exterior of the House of Caryatids is a non-verbal ironic note regarding the language of the decrees.

Pasternak calls it the 'House of Caryatids.' A caryatid is a building support or pillar in the shape of a woman. In his description he writes: 'This was the name of a dark grey steel-colour house with caryatids and statues of antique muses holding cymbals, lyres and masks decorating its façade' (p. 224). Could the fact that the arts supported the structure of the building be a metaphor for the role of the arts in life?

What is important to notice here is that both the theatre and the Party's Town Committee represent the complete opposite to the genuine private life in the house located *opposite* the House of Caryatids. In this house private lives, rich with meaning, compassion, understanding, love and caring for the other, thrive despite pressures of the life-threatening political upheaval surrounding Lara and Yurii in the street and at work. In these downright abnormal conditions, the love these two people have for each other is absolutely unique. After arriving from the forest and finding himself alone in Lara's apartment, becoming jealous of a possible relationship of Samdeviatov and Lara and wondering what Yurii could mean to her, he asks himself what Lara signifies to him and answers:

> Oh, that was easy! He knew that perfectly well.
>
> A spring evening ... the air is punctuated with scattered sounds. The voices of children playing in the streets come from varying distances as if to show the whole expanse is alive. The expanse is Russia, his incomparable mother; famed far and wide, martyred, stubborn, extravagant, crazy, irresponsible, adored, Russia with her eternally splendid, disastrous and unpredictable gestures. Oh, how sweet it was to be alive! How good to be alive and love life! And how he longed to thank life, thank existence itself; directly, face to face, to thank life in person.
>
> This is exactly what Lara was. You couldn't communicate with life, but she was its representative, its expression, the gift of speech and hearing granted to an inarticulate being (pp. 351-352).

What a poetic and unique image of a beloved! (No wonder so many girls have been named Lara!) How more *opposite* an image could one imagine to the images inhabiting the House of Caryatids, keeping in mind the trite style of the decrees Yurii read, just a while ago, on its outside walls! To justify the role of the title of this chapter, we could stop right here. But the author tries to contrast more than the content of these two buildings. In his description of the life of the city now, the days of the past and their spirit are still lingering in the background. Thus by allowing the reader a glimpse of the true past, the memory of which is being erased from the official present reality, he is trying to render a more truthful and informative picture of actuality.

The situation in the country and in Yuriatin is founded on lies, hiding the obvious truth and blaming the 'class of the haves' for hoarding food. We learn from Yurii's journey and his first encounter with Glafira that one does not tell the truth anymore about anything. She tells him not to speak about what he has seen on his way:

> "As I was saying, don't start telling anything at all. It is much better to keep your mouth shut. Credit co-operatives, luxury trains, inspection tours—forget about such things ... You could get into no end of trouble" (p. 347).

In this chapter we get a glimpse of the new reality in the small Siberian town. We learn that there are no passenger trains, since the railroads are used for freight trains that are moving food from Siberia to Moscow, one of the reasons why there is hardly any food left in Yuriatin. The ideology of the new rulers, the Bolsheviks, is built on their hatred of the 'class enemies.' Reason and common sense are nonexistent. This situation prevails in the school where Yurii is teaching, in the way the distribution of labour and food is managed and even in regard to former heroes like Strelnikov.

The above and many other phenomena of the time in the outside world are the complete *opposite* of the life that is experienced in the house *opposite* the House of Caryatids, the residence of the Party's Town Committee.

What makes the life in the house opposite the House of Caryatids different is that it is undiminishedly personal. Most of the description is conveyed in dialogues. The honest mutual openness between Yurii and Lara leads to unusual heartfelt closeness, which, in its turn, is reinforced by their complete isolation from hostile surroundings. A private life is experienced with all its happiness and conflicts, as is the powerlessness of individuals to decide their own fate in the face of history. Human weakness and the individual's choice of greatness are shown in the personal life and discussed in the context of religion and philosophy from a historic perspective.

The title of the chapter and the comparison of *these two houses* make one think about the possible meanings of the word opposite—'of the contrary kind,' 'diametrically different' *(Concise Oxford Dictionary)*. Again, it is the title that makes us think about the symbolic significance of these two opposite houses.

CHAPTER FOURTEEN: AGAIN VARYKINO

The first three sections of this chapter comment on the micro-climate of the political storm sweeping through Siberia in general and Yuriatin in particular. Komarovsky, on his way to the independent Mongolia, informs Lara and Yurii of the threats to their lives. He comes to offer them a place on the train he commands, which will take them to freedom. According to him, Lara's relationships with both Strelnikov and Zhivago are endangering her and Katya's lives. Thus, opening this chapter with events that have forced them to run from Yuriatin suggests that the same problems from which they are running will follow them to Varykino, into their refuge. Their hopes to survive for a while in Varykino, to escape the threats of the time, are completely unrealistic. The situation is clear to both of them, but they have no other place to which to run and they do not have much time left to be together. They cherish every moment and share their awareness thereof. It must be stressed that the location, Varykino, plays another important role in Yurii's life. It is the place where his creativity is inspired. If, as Zhivago tells Anna Ivanovna earlier in the novel, the only way we survive is in the memory of others, this visit to Varykino can be seen as the last celebration of their lives and, also, through the poems he will write here, a passage to eternal memory. It is here that Lara and Yurii celebrate the last moments of their love and it is here that Lara will be immortalized in his poetry. It is here, in Varykino, that he writes the poems which will survive both Yurii's and Lara's lives and will be cherished by his friends.

Already the first morning in Varykino Yurii is compelled to write. 'From the moment they got up, Yurii kept glancing at the table which stood so temptingly by the window. His fingers itched for paper and pen' (p. 386).

Zhivago also felt an urge to write when he arrived in Varykino for his first stay there. Although his first collection of poems, which already showed his talent, was published even before he returned from the war, the fruit of his pen, which appears at the end of the novel, according to the story of the novel, is written mostly in Varykino. (It is also mentioned there that some poems might have been written later in Moscow.) Thus, the poems by which he will be remembered are written in Varykino. During his first stay in this place he writes about his quest for understanding the nature of art and creativity. Now, only two years later, it is clear to both him and Lara that he has to write down all that he has created and keeps in his memory—his own art.

> "But as long as we have this breathing space, I want to ask you a favour. Will you give up a few hours in the next few evenings, and put down all the poems you have recited to me at different times? Half of them you've lost and the rest you have never written down and I am afraid you will forget them and they will be lost too, as you say has often happened to you before" (p. 390).

They both know that there is no future for them, their days are numbered, and on their minds as soon as they arrive in Varykino, apart from the basic necessities, are Zhivago's poems.

The complete creative process with all possible details is described in this chapter. The poet's moods, thoughts and even the dynamics of his handwriting, the titles of some the poems from the last chapter of the novel are mentioned here. It is also the most dynamic part of the plot considering the events that take place here, literally, their last days together, Lara's dramatic departure with Komarovsky, Zhivago's meeting and discussions with Strelnikov, the latter's suicide. In addition to all these events, the process of Yurii Zhivago's writing is described.

Gladkov, with all his negative criticism of the novel, probably due to the political situation at the time, writes about the material appearing at the Varykino location: 'All that is said about nature is excellent. The same about art. And about the process of composing poems.' [Without those pages, no researcher of Pasternak's poetry is able to manage, AM.]

The majority of those pages belong to the two chapters of the novel taking place in Varykino. Thus, also according to Gladkov, the entire process of creativity, vital in the understanding of Pasternak's poetry, is to be found in this chapter.

Moreover, Varykino is the place where real life blossoms as well as it provides a refuge from the problems of the time in history. The reader is offered a glance at Yurii's writing of both aspects of time, first in the form of a diary, secondly through the poems. Thus, his creativity, his writing, becomes a refuge from the historic time: 'Which, my dears, / Millennium, do we have here [in the yard]?' (B. Pasternak).

In this chapter the unique love story of the novel comes to the most extraordinary denouement. With Lara lost to both of them, Pasha, her husband and Yurii, her lover, their love for her is communicated here in a wonderfully moving conversation taking place between the two of them. As they share their cherished memories of her, the unexpected happens and it seems that their love for her brings these two rivals closer to each other.

In the preceding chapter Yurii defines what Lara means to him, by describing what Russia signifies to him, seeing them both as the quintessence of his life, his existence.

Lara is also the cause for Strelnikov volunteering his service to the Russian army, whole-heartedly dedicating himself to the October Revolution and fighting for it in the civil war. He justifies his cruelty when fighting in the civil war as necessary in the cleansing of the unjust and corrupt Russia, as revenge for all the wrongs that were perpetrated on the Russian people. His motivation to fight is inspired by the image of the offended Lara. Thus, for Strelnikov, Lara and Russia merge and are reflected, in his perception, in Lara's face.

> [T]he watchfulness, the disquiet of those days—it was all there, you could read it all in her face, in her eyes. Everything that made that time what it was—the tears and the insults and the hopes, the whole accumulation of revenge and pride, it was all in her expression in her carriage in that mixture of girlish shyness and grace and daring. You could indict the century in her name, out of her mouth (p. 412).

When Yurii tells him that he, too, saw Lara at that time and that Strelnikov described extremely well what one could see in Lara's face, Strelnikov asks him:

> "You saw and you remembered? And what did you do about it?" Yurii answers: "That's another answer altogether" (p. 413).

Yurii and Strelnikov are in love with the same woman, they both deeply love the same country. Their love, however, causes them to act in different ways. Strelnikov does not know what this love elicits in Yurii's behaviour, nor is he able to appreciate what Yurii does. Likewise, Yurii does not approve of or understands what Strelnikov and people like him do. At the time Strelnikov arrives in Varykino, Yurii has done what he knows best. Yurii is a poet and he immortalizes Lara and the country he loves in his poetry:

I'll write your memory into an image of infinite pain and grief ... This is how I will trace your image. I will trace it on paper as the sea, after a fearful storm has churned it up to its foundations, leaves the traces of the strongest, furthest-reaching wave on the shore ... This is how you were cast in my life, my love, my pride, this is how I will write about you (pp. 404-405).

The two men also act differently in their love for Russia. Strelnikov acts out of anger. He needs revenge. Strelnikov fights with the sword, Yurii with the pen—he believes that the pen is mightier than the sword. He searches for an answer, he needs to understand what has happened to his country, to its people. When he understands, he fights with the pen (like Pasternak). Strelnikov kills himself; Yurii continues to live and with all the hardship remains a free-thinking individual fighting for justice in his beloved country.

As noticed before, along with the story of individual lives, the novel provides a historical commentary on Russia during the time described in the novel. In this chapter, Zhivago finalizes his position vis-à-vis the October Revolution, not in a discussion with an opponent but in internal dialogue with himself. Or, is it also with Tolstoy?:

The forest does not change its place, we cannot lie in wait for it and catch it in the act of moving. However much we look at it we see it as motionless. And such is also the immobility in our eyes of the eternal growing, ceaseless changing of life, of society, of history moving as invisibly in its incessant transformation as the forest in spring.

Tolstoy thought in just this way but did not say in so many words. While denying that history is set in motion by Napoleon or any other ruler or general he did not carry his reasoning to conclusion. History is not made by anyone. You cannot make history; nor can you see history anymore than you can see grass growing. Wars and revolutions, kings and Robespierres, are history's organic agents, its yeast. *But revolutions are made by fanatical men of action with one-track minds, man who are narrow-minded on the point of genius. They overturn the old order in a few hours or days; the whole upheaval takes a few weeks or at the most years, but for decades thereafter, for centuries, the spirit of narrowness which led to the upheaval is worshiped as holy* (p. 406).

It is worth pointing out that the editorial committee of Novy Mir did not mention the above italicized lines when accusing Pasternak of criticizing the October Revolution.

Zhivago feels it is his duty to understand what went wrong with the October Revolution. To find and tell the truth about the history of Russia during the described period seems to be the aim of Zhivago's and Pasternak's lives.

Thus, Varykino, the place of physical refuge, is most of all a spiritual refuge—it inspires creativity, it moves the poet from daily existence and constant inquiry to writing, to the place of eternal memory. It seems that Varykino does more than rhyme with Peredelkino, it makes one think about the role Peredelkino played in Pasternak's creative life.

CHAPTER FIFTEEN: CONCLUSION (THE END)

At first sight it does not appear that also this title is pointing to anything particular besides concluding the storyline of the protagonists. And what a conclusion it is! It is impossible to do justice to it, short of copying the whole text, since conveying the content would amount to retelling a poem. Zhivago's and Lara's lives come to an end as do many of the other major themes communicated in the novel. This chapter and the following epilogue are assigned an ordinal number, possibly for balance, since ordinal numbers are assigned to all the chapters including the one containing Zhivago's poems. The chapters thus are made equal as far as concerns the form, the structure and content of the novel.

The many different endings (or conclusions) in this chapter follow the impressionistic style of the novel and metaphorically convey the situation during the period between the beginning of The New Economic Plan (NEP) up to 1929. Thus, Vasya Brykin's fate represents that of children orphaned by the Civil War and of other village people who succeeded in the Soviet system by embracing its ideology uncritically. Gordon's and Dudorov's experiences and way of thinking represent the new Soviet intelligentsia, people brutally brainwashed by the system, to a point that they idealize its cruel and unjust demands. Dvornik Markel's place in this new society and the opportunities opened to Marina and other members of his family, show the negative and positive changes that are woven into the social fabric with the new system in place.

When Zhivago and Vasia enter Moscow this time, they come from the east. Like at the end of chapter five, Yurii sees the Cathedral of Christ the Saviour, which will soon be destroyed by Stalin's orders, and all the golden cupolas of the city; this view is a concealed end to the old Moscow, the face of the city that existed before it became Moscow of the time the novel was written. Pasternak describes Yurii's last journey riding the tram:

> He had no luck with the tram ... The luckless tram was stuck for the twentieth time ... Yurii felt sick and faint. Overcoming his weakness, he got up and jerked the window straps up and down trying to open the window, but he could not move it.
> People shouted to him that the window was blocked, it was nailed in position, but Yurii fighting off his faintness seized by a sort of panic (pp. 437-438).

The disrepair of the tram, the nailed-down windows of the tram that he cannot open, the lack of air, all is an obvious metaphor for the situation in Russia. The grey-haired lady, noticed by Yurii from his window running ahead of the tram when it stopped and then falling behind when it moved, reminds Yurii of school problems and makes him wonder:

> 'He thought of several people whose lives run parallel and close together but at different speed, and wondered in what circumstances some of them would overtake the others. Something like a theory of relativity applied to human race-course occurred to him' (p. 438).

Mademoiselle Fleury gets her permit to leave Russia to go home to freedom the same day Yurii dies choking from lack of air. This is the end of Yurii's life and a metaphoric representation of the social predicament in Russia. Pasternak shows here these two lives, different in all aspects (age, nationality, individuality), in the human race-course where

Yurii, the Russian uncompromising, free individual, loses the race to the self-absorbed Mademoiselle Fleury, who is utterly well adjusted to different political situations. The race between Russia, represented by the quandary of the tram, and Mademoiselle Fleury can be seen as a metaphor for the situation in Russia and the indifference shown by western visitors and celebrities towards Russia's predicament.

It is also in this chapter that Zhivago has his final disagreements with his friends and openly criticizes life under the Soviet system which they support:

> It's the common illness of the time. I think its causes are chiefly moral. The great majority of us are required to live a life of constant, systematic duplicity. Your health is bound to be affected if, day after day, you say the opposite of what you feel, if you grovel before what you dislike and rejoice at what brings you nothing but misfortune (p. 432).

Yurii's dramatic death, which in symbolic terms could be seen as the end of the free Russian intelligentsia, followed by Lara's disappearance soon after Yurii's death to a labour camp, weep not only for the end of the breathtaking, unique love story, but also for the end of justice and freedom in Soviet society. Yurii's death symbolizes the fate of a free-thinking individual in this new society. Lara's fate clearly represents the cruel reality for other free individuals in those same times.

> She must have been arrested in the street, as so often happened in those days, and she died or vanished somewhere, forgotten as a nameless number on a list which later was mislaid, in one of the innumerable mixed-women concentration camps in the north (p. 449).

What is happening at Yurii's funeral is full of subtle but noteworthy hints about the situation in the country. Whatever takes place there, however, loses in importance, beauty, meaning in poetic prose, and more, when compared to Lara's arrival at the funeral and her last farewell to Yurii (p. 447). The spirit of the whole novel is poetically rendered in these few pages (pp. 439-448). Lara's parting words to Yurii are so moving, so unusual, considering that he is dead, so poetic that one hesitates to invest in them collateral interpretations however easy and tempting that may be.

The lives of both protagonists are described in this chapter. What follows in the novel after their deaths is without them, although they survive in the memory of people who knew them. Their memory triumphs in Zhivago's poems, collected and published by Evgraf. Yurii's thoughts and ideas presented in his poems becomes a source of inspiration for hope of a better future and for freedom for his friends and others. Also Lara and Yurii's love for her survive in these poems.

This chapter ends with Yurii's funeral, the third funeral in the novel. In a novel that celebrates life, love and dedication to freedom, each of the three funerals in the novel symbolically buries a period along with the person buried. The first funeral, with the singing of 'Eternal Memory,' opens the novel. It is the funeral of Yurii's mother and it also marks the end of Yurii's childhood. At the second funeral of Anna Ivanovna, Yurii loses his adopted mother. More than anything else, however, her funeral symbolizes the end of an epoch in the history of Russia. It is the last funeral that invokes religion and tradition. The third funeral, that of Yurii Zhivago, is Soviet style, and it also symbolizes the end of an era and the beginning of a new. The time period that follows is left out of the novel and is barely mentioned subsequently in the novel. Chronologically, the third funeral brings us to the end of the twenties. It is worth mentioning here that in his *Autobiographical Outline*, published in 1957, Pasternak, in reference to by and large the same year, writes:

> To continue it further would have been inordinately difficult. Keeping to the (chronological) sequence, further, one would have to speak about years, circumstances, people and fates, stricken by the frame of the revolution., about a world of goals earlier unknown, tasks and exploits, new restraints, new strictness and new ordeals, which this world presented to the *human individual, honor and pride, industry and endurance of a human being.*

In this same writing Pasternak also points out *how* one should write about this period: 'It has to be written in a way that the heart should stop beating and the hair should raise/stand up on one's head ... We are still far from that ideal'.

'We' in this case could be Pasternak himself and/or the literature of his time.

Taking into account all that was said, as well as the historical period that descended on the country later, the title of this chapter could be seen as the end of a period in the history of Russia. The time that followed had no place for people like Yurii and Lara or for most people of their kind.

CHAPTER SIXTEEN: THE EPILOGUE

It is fourteen years since Yurii died. It is the summer of 1943, over two years for Russia into World War II. Gordon, recently promoted to lieutenant, and Major Dudorov meet in a small Russian town. As they are surrounded by the devastation caused by the war, Misha Gordon's behaviour triggers an exchange of stories from their lives in the years that passed since we last saw them together. In a most condensed yet informative style we are told about the years that followed Yurii's death. We learn about the politicized atmosphere at Soviet universities from an original love relationship between Dudorov, the professor, and Christina Orletsova, his student. She later became a war hero when she courageously sacrificed her life to save fellow soldiers. We learn about the Soviet justice system, its jails, concentration camps. The atmosphere in the penal system is most powerfully conveyed in the following lines:

> "They called our company the death squad. It was practically wiped out. How and why I survived, I don't know. And yet—imagine—all the utter hell was nothing, it was bliss compared to the horrors of the concentration camp, and not because of the material conditions, but for some other reasons" (pp. 452-453).

And Inokentii, with better luck during those years, agrees:

> "It isn't only in comparison with your life as a convict, but compared to everything in the thirties, even to my

favourable conditions at the university, in the midst of books and money and comfort; even to me there, the war came as a breath of fresh air, an omen of deliverance, a purifying storm" (p. 453).

Their discussion, very different from the last one they had with Yurii in the previous chapter, shows that their education and reeducation, about which Dudorov spoke to Yurii and Gordon in their last meeting, were lost. They now think and speak as individuals and do not ruminate as before about Soviet slogans. Seeing reality from their own point of view, they look back also at collectivization as another catastrophic mistake of Stalin's rule:

"I think that collectivization was both a mistake and failure, and, because that couldn't be admitted, every means of intimidation had to be used to make people forget how to think and judge for themselves, to force them to see what wasn't there, and to maintain the contrary of what their eyes told them. Hence the unexampled harshness of the Yezhov terror, and the promulgation of a constitution which was never intended to be applied, and the holding of elections not based on the principle of free vote.

"And when the war broke out, its real horrors, its real dangers, its menace of real death, were a blessing compared with the inhuman power of the lie, a relief because it broke the *spell of the dead letter*"(p. 453).

Tanka, the laundry girl, is Yurii and Lara's daughter here in the new Russia. As mentioned in the analysis of the preceding chapter, Pasternak did not dare write about the years that followed Yurii and Lara's death. Tanka's story and the Russian language she speaks illustrate what those years have done to Russia and its culture. After listening to Tanka's story, Yurii's friends realize that she is Yurii and Lara's daughter. Her parents, two enlightened representatives of the Russian intelligentsia, belonged to the same social class as Gordon and Dudorov. Gordon's response clearly shows his position regarding the revolution and the changes it brought to Russia:

> "This has happened several times in the course of history. A thing that has been conceived in a lofty, ideal manner becomes coarse and material. Thus Rome came out of Greece and the Russian Revolution came out of Russian enlightenment" (p. 463).

The experience of the years that followed Yurii's death changed the way Dudorov and Gordon were thinking in the present. They were thinking as free individuals; they had their own opinions.

The novel ends with an optimistic outlook. His friends nourish their hope with a booklet of Zhivago's poems that they are reading. They yearn for a clearing in the political atmosphere, for freedom of thought and expression in their beloved country.

The conclusion, the previous chapter, ended with Yurii and Lara's death. Now in the epilogue the memory of them crosses the border between life and death and enters eternity through this collection of Yurii's poems.

The free individual, represented in this novel by Yurii Zhivago, who refuses to compromise the truth at the high price of losing everything dear and important to him, becomes the source of hope and rehabilitation for his friends. His friends can be seen as a metaphor for other Russian people who learned from their experience. Thus, freedom of the individual, the right to think and act freely, is shown to be essential for life. The freedom of thought and expression, the freedom to be oneself, is shown here as the *a priori* condition for the growth of freedom in the family, in the country and in the world.

Skaz and Stream of Consciousness

In reviewing the two parts of *Doctor Zhivago* we have shown how the titles, the method—priom—and the author's point of view interact to convey implicit messages in the text of the novel. The structural role of the titles is directed towards the true content of the chapters. In commenting on the next part of the work we have shown how the priom Pasternak employs in the presentation of a character, a theme and an episode adheres to the principles of the leitmotif of the novel—namely, it avoids didacticism in every possible way in order to refrain from imposing on the reader any particular point of view.

Here we examine how also the stylization of the narrative is devised to convey information collateral to what is overtly presented in the text. Before we proceed in this direction, it is of interest to consider Pasternak's opinion regarding the relationship between content and form. According to his memoirs, the following passage describing his thoughts as a young poet was written soon after he finished writing *Doctor Zhivago*:

> Quite the contrary, the subject matter [content, AM] of my poems was my constant preoccupation, my constant dream was that my poem itself should have something in it, that it should have a new idea or a new picture, that it should be engraved with all its peculiarities in the book and should speak from its pages with its silence and with all the colors of its black colorless print (*I Remember*).

Although this passage describes Pasternak's convictions at the time of writing his early poems, in *Doctor Zhivago* he adheres to the same principle as concerns the details and the novel as a whole.

In *Doctor Zhivago* Pasternak discusses form twice. In the first instance the example is drawn from life:

> He was still wearing his school cup. It slithered continually from his bandaged head and, instead of taking it off and carrying it in his hand, he rammed it back each time, disturbing the bandage and the wound, and in this the two guards assisted him with readiness.
>
> *There was something symbolical in this absurd action, so contrary to common sense*, and, impressed by its significance, Yurii longed to rush out and address the boy in words which were boiling up inside him. He longed to shout to him and the people in the railway coach that *salvation lay not in loyalty to forms and uniforms, but in throwing them away* (p. 224).

This passage is a representation of many situations in life. It is unmistakably a clear, visual illustration of Zhivago's thought and Pasternak's principle.

Several pages later the more particular role of form in art is discussed:

> I have always thought that *art* is not a category, not a realm in which there are innumerable concepts and varied phenomena, but that, on the contrary, it is something concentrated, strictly limited. It is a principle which comes into every work of art, a force applied to it and a truth worked out in it. *And I have never seen it as form but rather as a hidden, secret part of content* (p. 256).

According to the above quotes, content comes first in

the hierarchy of importance in art and, at best, form can be a secret part of the content. Thus, being singularly faithful to form limits freedom in life, art, while form may reveal a hidden aspect, subserving content. As shown already in our analysis, this is clearly the case in this novel.

In order to reach more deeply into the content of the novel, it serves us to be aware that the form of the work is governed by its content, that the form is an inseparable modality of its content. As in sign language, the form of the work conveys necessary additional information to the verbal content. Such thoughts were on Pasternak's (Zhivago's) mind, as we read in the following passage:

> Another thing is that I am obsessed by the problem of mimicry, of mimesis, the outward adaption of an organism to the color of its environment. I think it throws an astonishing light on *the relationship of the inward and outward world* (p. 366). [Conversion, transformation ... of the inward to the outward, AM.]

Here we will pay attention to the stylization of the narrative in the novel. The above passage is revelatory in this regard.

The stylistic range of the narrative is wide. In addition to a third person narration in the author's voice, the novel presents *dialogues; stream of consciousness; vernacular variations,* e.g., in the expressions of Markel and Galuzina, Svirid and others; *notes*, by, for instance, Lara and Nina Kologrivova (pp. 74, 342); *letters*, as by Tonia and Yurii (pp. 123, 124, 373-374); *diaries* by Vedeniapin and Zhivago (pp. 48-49, 252-261, 436); *folk language and versification* in the cases of Kubarikha and Galuzina (244, 327); *skaz,* e.g., in words by Panfil Palykh, the man with the stump in the forest, Vasya Brykin and Tanka the laundry maid (pp. 315, 332, 421, 459); *dreams,* Lara's and Zhivago's (pp. 53, 257, 353-354); *passages from newspapers, decrees, declaration* (pp. 116, 339-340, 343); *oratory*, exemplified by Gintz and Vlas Galuzin (pp. 129-130, 291-292); and last, but prominently, Yurii Zhivago's poems.

The relationship between stylistic form and content is more obvious in some cases than in others. Here we will contemplate this connection in some of the examples mentioned. For instance, the skaz of Panfil Palykh expresses a *folklore stylization*:

> "They say a tale is soon told. But my story is a long one. I couldn't tell it all in three years. I don't know where to begin…" (p. 315).
> "Now, I'll tell you the whole truth if you want it, I'll say it in your face but you mustn't hold it against me" (p. 316).

In Russian these quotes sound like something coming from a folktale and in Panfil's language, along with them, Soviet jargon and slogans are found, e.g., 'soldiers of the world revolution,' 'down your rifles,' 'go home,' 'turn against the bourgeois' (p. 315).

Reading Panfil's story carefully, we realize that he is sly and that he avoids the truth at first. He has assumed the pose of a *muzhik* (simple peasant) who has been enlightened by the war and the revolution. His speech, stylized in short sentences in a certain rhythm, is reminiscent of propaganda style slogans. Panfil has consciously organized his manner of speaking to correspond to the role he has chosen to play. He first tells his story in a very general way. He talks about the revolution and how he joined the partisans, as ordinary facts of those times and as consequences of historical events (beyond his control). Lajos's definition of Panfil as a conscientious man with innate class instinct is consistent with Panfil's own words. In the second part of his story Panfil steps out of this role and tells Zhivago the whole truth. Even when doing so, however, the rhythm and language of his story is not an authentic voice but rather one with an adopted vernacular:

> "I've done away with a lot of your kind, there's a lot of officers' blood on my hands. Officers, gentry. And it never worried me. Spilt like water" (p. 316).

The repetitions, the metaphors and in general the style of his monologue do not sound as Panfil's normal way of expressing himself but more like a literary, embellished speech. In his tone there is self-justification and self-respect for his past achievements, which his organized linguistic style represents well. Trying to hide the main reason for his 'creeps' speaks for his lack of sincerity. Also lacking in his story are the people who were the cause behind his decision to join the partisans. The patriotic past is well known history, his main concern now is his family. His choice of language when he talks to Zhivago reveals a certain political slyness. When he speaks about the cruelties he has committed, he speaks about them in general, in plural numbers and as facts with which the doctor is supposed to be familiar. When he tells about the cruelties committed by the enemy or his concerns for his family, however, the description of the atrocities is in an altogether different style:

> "He'll get hold of my wife and he'll tie her up and he will start tormenting her on my account; he will torture my wife and my children; he'll brake every bone in their bodies; he'll tear them apart" (p. 316).

In conclusion, Panfil's character is revealed in his style, and since Panfil represents many people like him, the skaz style conveys not only Panfil's cruelty but also that of his time. The bleeding stump of a man describes the cruelties of the White enemy. Like Panfil, he uses a vocabulary and style that remind of a folklore tale:

> "The whole town is growling. They boil people alive. They cut strips out of them" (p. 331).
> [This is a more literal translation of the Russian original text than the one published, AM.]

In the last moments a person about to be killed is overwhelmed by pain and fear. There is more cruelty of this time in history conveyed in this short fragment than in any exhaustive descriptions of the war and war actions. The unfortunate victim of the civil war is warning the partisans. He addresses them as brothers. His vocabulary as well as the rhythm of his language sound like the last words of a lost soul. His speech is not well organized and is not premeditated as Panfil's speech. Both he and Panfil, however, are actors in this catastrophic civil war and to convey the cruelties of the times the skaz style they share in their stories is very fitting. In the agony of the civil war both Panfil and the bleeding stump of a man have at least a say in their choice of action, which nevertheless ends tragically for them.

In the following two skazs a different story is told. Vasya, a young boy, not only is the victim of circumstances caused by political and historical events but he also represents innocent victims of individual human dishonesty. His uncle has run away, leaving him as hostage on the train. Kharlam settles his score with Pelgea by punishing an innocent Vasya. He takes his revenge on the village and Vasya when Pelgea is already dead. In Vasya's story we hear about events that happen in 'peace time,' when there is already a stable government, and it was collecting from the village a 'surplus' above the government allotment. Whatever takes place here is of a personal nature. The deeds of Kharlam, the widow with her potatoes, the drunk Red army soldiers, the fire and the horrors that followed—they are all manifestations of human weakness. And Vasya himself, who blames Kharlam in the beginning of the catastrophe, concludes, without substantiated information, that: "What came after happened of itself. Nobody arranged it, nobody's to blame" (p. 422).

Vasya's skaz, like the previous, has a conclusion. It ends at the same point of time-space with which it started. The burned, deserted village, where the doctor meets Vasya, is all Vasya finds when he comes out of his refuge. It is important to note that Vasya's story is preceded by two other references to this burned-down village. The first time we learn about the fate of the village is when Zhivago meets Pelgea on the 'highway.' According to her information:

> Veretenniki has been raided in reprisal for withholding food supplies. It was said that Vasya's house has been burned down and that a member of his family has perished (p. 300).

The second time, before Vasya's story, the village is described by the narrator:

> The burned down ruins were those of his [Vasya's] native village, Veretenniki. His mother was dead. When the village was destroyed, Vasya hid in the cave... (p. 419).

These two versions preceding the story told by Vasya show us how the skaz conveys the same events in a form in which the cruelties forcefully seize the reader's mind. Vasya's story, framed as a skaz, conveys the same story but in a style that engages the reader differently. The way Vasya tells the story, the reader could imagine becoming a victim of the events Vasya describes, because, according to Vasya, the events were spontaneous acts of human failure, not planned ahead of time and not imposed by any government.

Vasya, who experienced all the cruelty of his time at an early age, comes to Moscow with the doctor and soon finds his place in the new Soviet society. Zhivago, who helped him organize his life, is left behind by Vasya who soon joins the new life and embraces its values:

> The obviousness, the self-evidence of the truth proclaimed by the revolution attracted him increasingly, and Yuri's talk with its obscurities and its imagery, now struck him as the voice of error, doomed, conscious of its weakness and therefore evasive (p. 425).

    This passage describes not only the direction Vasya's life is taking but also stresses that the doctor's language becomes an obstacle for Vasya to understand him. Vasya's failure to understand Zhivago's language is a metaphor for the disrespect that the young generation harbours for the values of the past when adopting the ideas and new values of Soviet society.

    The change of values and culture is represented here by the change in language. Thus, the way language is used by the different generations of dissimilar ideologies expresses their divergence. The short quote above uses language as a metaphor to represent the dynamics of political and cultural changes in the country. Zhivago's language separates him from Vasya, who represents the future generation that has integrated itself with the new life. This role assigned to language in the novel becomes even more evident with the last skaz, which concludes the last chapter of the novel and is told by the laundry woman Tanka, who turns out to be Yuri and Lara's daughter.

    Tanka's skaz is the longest of them all. Gordon and Dudorov are shocked that this young woman is Yuri and Lara's daughter. *Tanka's language* and the events of which she speaks with them belong to a world that is alien to any civilized society. According to the chronology of the novel, Tanka could not have been born before 1922, and, given the events she describes, her birth took place during the NEP period. Hence she could not have been more than six years old when the robber appeared. If indeed, as we soon find out, Tanka is Yuri and Lara's daughter, both of them being members of the Russian intelligentsia that preceded the Revolution, her *language* leaves us with a more tragic impression than do the disastrous events she describes.

The language Tanka speaks becomes an analogy to the tragedy that took place for an entire generation of neglected children, victims of the civil war and also victims of Soviet Russia. Tanka is now twenty-one years old. It is two years since the war started. She left Aunt Marfa at the age of six. Who is responsible for what happened in her life? Tanka's language represents the failure of the Soviet system, since, from the age of six, she was subject to its decisions and actions. It is not by chance that after having listened to her story Gordon concludes:

> This has happened several times in the course of history. A thing which has been conceived in a lofty, ideal manner became coarse and material. Thus Rome came out of Greece and the Russian Revolution came out of the Russian enlightenment (p. 463).

All the above-mentioned skazs stand on their own merit without any mediation of the author's voice. They are organically entwined with the literary styles of the text. Each one of them has its unique, personal language, defined by the vocabulary and the manner in which they communicate. Gordon's story about his time in a gulag and later on in the war (p. 452) is not included here, although, if classified by content alone, it could have been. But Gordon's language is not original and belongs to the same category as the narrator's language. Gordon does not speak in the first person singular but in the less personal plural 'we.' The last time we heard Gordon speak before, he was in the company of Zhivago and Dudorov—at the time Gordon lost his own individuality and voice. He admires everything hackneyed and Soviet. Gordon is thus a different kind of victim from the people in the above skazs. Pasternak shows him in a different position. Unlike other victims, Gordon believes in and contributes to the regime of which he soon becomes a victim. This differentiation in the victims of the regime (Strelnikov is another case) is another silent reproach by the author to those who quickly lost their individuality.

> "We were unlucky. We were sent to just about the worst of punitive camps ... First we broke saplings with our bare hands in the frost, to get wood to build our huts with" (p. 452).

No personal point of view is offered, no expression of personal pain, just historical facts.

The episodes of the first four skazs are told by victims and are characterized by a language of individual vocabulary and rhythm. They are telling their story from the point of view of a victim and their language is clearly the spoken language. Maybe Tynyanov's definition of the skaz helps to appreciate their function in the text:

> The skaz makes the word *felt physiologically*. The whole story becomes a monologue, it's addressed to every reader—the reader enters the story, starts to intone, to gesticulate, smile, he does not read the story but plays it.

We do not play the story, but we feel it. We do not smile, but we cry with it. The events are all connected to the period when the country is experiencing extremely hard times and their presentation in the form of a skaz are therefore 'felt physiologically.' This becomes even more evident when we look at other forms of stylization and the relationship of form with content in other cases.

The fact that the Christian motif is absent from the skazs does not seem to be accidental. We do not find the mentioning of God or the asking for His intervention or help. Yet elsewhere in the novel an important place is given to the Christian motif. It is true that it does not appear in its traditional form, but already in the first pages of the novel the Christian motif emerges at the core of the philosophy of Nikolay Vedenyapin (p. 19) and also in the last pages of the novel in the poetry of Yurii Zhivago. Between these two points one can find a number of instances where God is mentioned in a meaningful context, like in the following:

> Lara was not religious. She did not believe in ritual. But sometimes, to enable her to bear her life, she needed the accompaniment of an inward music and she could not always compose herself. That music was God's word of life and it was to weep over it that she went to church (p. 53).

And later in her life we hear her say:

> "From what Yurii told me they had a long conversation."
> "Is it really true! Well *thank God, thank God*, that's better."
> Antipova slowly crossed herself. "What an astounding, what a preordained [*from above*, AM] coincidence" (pp. 443-444).

We also find that Lara is well familiar with the ritual and that she regrets that Zhivago is not being buried according to the church ritual:

> She thought: "All the same, what a pity he isn't having a church funeral. The burial service is so splendid and tremendous! It's more than most people deserve when

they die, but darling Yurii would have been such a noble occasion!" (p. 446).

The last skaz on our list belongs to Tanka. It ends on the last page of the prose text of the novel. In Tanka's skaz we find not Christian motifs but rather pagan ones, motifs found in early Christian literature in Russia, when remnants of paganism were still upheld by the people:

"No sooner had I thought this than I heard Udaloy neighing outside; he had been standing out there in the yard ready all the time. Yes, that was how it was. Udaloy was neighing as much as to say: 'Let's fly quickly, Tanya, and find some good people and get some help.' I looked out of the window and saw that it was getting near dawn. 'All right,' I thought, 'thank you for putting the thought into my head, Udaloy. So be it. We'll go.' But hardly have I thought this when again I heard as if it were a voice calling from the wood: 'Wait, don't hurry, Tanya, we'll do it in another way.' Again I knew I wasn't alone in the wood. An engine hooted down below, like a cock crowing in our own yard... 'Am I off my head,' I wondered, 'like Auntie Marfa, that every living beast and every dumb engine speaks to me in plain Russian?' " (pp. 461-462).

What Pasternak points to here can be associated with the description of pagan Rome by Vedenyapin (pp. 48-49) and with Gordon's conclusion after having heard Tanya's story (p. 463). The elements of pagan culture, the location, the language and the tone of her story together create the form that corresponds to the content of her story. In both Gordon's comment and in Blok's poem (quoted by Gordon after listening to the story) the remote plural voice used here, in accord with Tanka's skaz, is Pasternak's commentary about the civilization of the country at this historical time. 'Thus

Rome came out of Greece' (p. 463).

At the other end of the scale regarding stylization in the novel, we find the form closest to the 'stream of consciousness.' We see it in the introduction to Galuzina in chapter ten and, in adding another aspect to Yurii's character, in chapter thirteen. These two characters belong to different social strata in life and yet the same type of stylization is used to emphasize certain core issues in their characters. Looking closely at these issues, we find that the connection between form and content in them is of the same kind. We also notice the same stylistic preamble for the stream of consciousness in both cases.

Before Galuzina's stream of consciousness begins, the time and place of her whereabouts are described. Thus before we are introduced to Galauzina's thoughts, we have already read about a barking and chained puppy named Tomik and a cawing crow and that they both could be heard all over town. In the description of Galuzina's path, the dog Tomik is mentioned again, when, after her walk, Galuzina arrives at the entrance of her home. Information about the time is then added: "At the seventh hour of the church's reckoning, and at one in the morning by the clock… that this was…'the night of Maundy Thursday.'" A quarter of an hour later Galuzina appears. She left the monastery because she didn't feel well. The cause of her worries was her son Teryoshka, who has been affected by the mobilization order posted that day. The posters about the mobilization order accompanies her all the way. Galuzina is introduced by the narrator:

> The stormy sadness of her thoughts oppressed her. Here she tried to think them all out aloud, one by one, she would not have had sufficient words or time enough till dawn. But out here in the street, these comfortless reflections flew at her in clusters, and she could deal with all of them together, in a short while it took her to walk a few times from the monastery gate

to the corner of the square and back (p. 279).

The above remarks inform us regarding the place and time her thoughts occur.

When examining Galuzina's thoughts, the vocabulary and syntax of which differ from those of the narrator's, we find that they are propelled by the most essential issues in her life. Switching from the narrator's thoughts to Galuzina's, the author does not use quotation marks, since the transition is obvious given her vocabulary and diction:

> It was almost Eastertide and there was not a soul in the house; they had all gone away, leaving her alone. Well, wasn't she alone? Of course she was. Her ward Ksyusha didn't count. Who was she anyway? 'Another soul is a dark pool,' as the saying goes. Perhaps she was a friend, or perhaps she was an enemy or a secret rival. She was supposed to be the daughter of her husband's first wife by another marriage. Her husband Vlas said he had adopted her. But suppose she was his natural daughter? Or suppose she wasn't his daughter at all but something else? Could you ever see into a man's heart? Though, to Katyusha her due, there was nothing wrong with her. She had brains, looks, manners—much more brains than either poor stupid Teryoshka or his father! (pp. 279-280).

This short passage gives the quintessence of Galuzina's family relationships or, more precisely, Galuzina's thoughts about faithfulness and jealousy, two essential feelings in family dynamics. She has lived for years with her husband's adopted daughter and, although she can objectively see Ksycha's beauty and talents, being upset about her doubts regarding Vlas and Ksyusha's relationship, she thinks through all the negative possibilities from Ksyusha being his illegitimate daughter to being Galuzina's rival.

We read further that:

> Vlas was gallivanting up and down the highway, making speeches to the new recruits, exhorting them to mighty feats of arms. Instead of looking after his own son, the fool, and saving him from mortal peril! (p. 280).

Teryoshka is the most loved person in her life, and all the time she returns to him in her thoughts by comparing him with Ksyusha, by worrying about his safety, accusing his father of doing nothing for his son's safety or remembering what happened to Teryoshka at school: "The poor lad has been expelled from school..." (p. 280). Galuzina is depressed. *The mobilization order, which affects Teryoshka's life, is the main cause of her misery.* She is looking for the cause that brought her to her present predicament and blames the mobilization for everything:

> What has caused all this misery? Was it the revolution? No, oh no! It was the war. The war has killed off the flower of Russian manhood, and now there was nothing but rotten, good-for-nothing rubbish left (p. 280).

Speaking about the flower of Russian manhood, she goes back to memories of her youth, when she lived in her father's house along with her sister Olya:

> And master carpenters had called on their father, everyone a fine outstanding figure of a man... And everything in those days had been fine and rich and seemly—church services and dances and people and manners—everything had rejoiced her heart, for all that her family had been simple people who came of peasant and worker stock (p. 280).

Galuzina is turning over in her mind the years of her girlhood, the happiest years of her life. She comes back to them when she thinks about the 'results' of the mobilizations—the ruin of all the 'flower of manhood.' Although her father has achieved a good position in the city life, she is not forgetting her roots—peasants and workers. Her thoughts move from her own youth to what those years meant in the life of Russia then and now:

> *And Russia too was a marriageable girl in those days*, courted by real men, men who would stand up for her, not to be compared with this rabble nowadays. Now everything has lost its gloss, nothing but civilians left, lawyers and Yids clacking their tongues day and night. Poor old Vlas and his friends thought they could bring back those golden days by toasts and speeches and good wishes! But was this the way to win back a lost love? (p. 280).

Comparing the best years of her life—her years of girlhood with Russia's 'girlhood,' Galuzina pays homage to the omitted in both cases. Not saying openly that the master carpenters were courting her and her sister, she speaks about Russia being courted by real men. Likewise when she criticizes Vlas's behavior in relation to Russia, she thinks about his relation towards her. *Thus, Galuzina's fate and the fortunes of the country are interwoven in her thoughts to the point of completely blending into each other.* The happiness of both is contingent on their admirers and their defenders. The last concept is closely connected to that of the conscription, which dominates her thoughts. Here her stream of consciousness ends. As mentioned before, this chapter is not enclosed in quotation marks but differs considerably from the vocabulary and syntax of the narrator.

In the following chapter the narrator's voice intrudes. At first he describes Galuzina's route:

The market-place was the size of a large field. In times gone by, it had been crowded on market days with peasants' carts. At one end of it was St. Helen Street (Yeleninskaya): the other, curving in a crescent, was lined with small buildings, one or two storeys high, used for warehouses, offices and shops (p. 281).

After describing the market square, Pasternak continues its description in a way that mixes Galuzina's vocabulary with that of the narrator. To the description of those places he also adds Galuzina's feelings and memories:

There, she remembered, in more peaceful times, Bryukhanov, a cross old bear in spectacles and long frock coat, who dealt in leather, oats and hay, cartwheels and harness, would read the penny paper as he sat importantly on a chair outside his great, fourfold iron doorway.
And there, in a small dim window, a few pairs of beribboned wedding candles ... thousands of rouble deals were made by unknown agents of a millionaire candle manufacturer who lived nobody knew where.
There, in the middle of the row of shops, was the Galuzin's large grocery store with three windows... And there Galuzina, as a young married woman, had often and willingly sat behind the cash desk. Her favourite colour was violet-mauve, the colour of church vestments on certain solemn days, the colour of lilac in bud, the colour of her best velvet dress and of her set of crystal goblets. It was the colour of happiness and of her memories, and Russia, too, in her virginity before the revolution, seemed to her to have the colour of lilac (p. 281).

The places come alive. People, colours, life start to move into the dark street she is walking. Stressing the emotions and feelings Galuzina has for this place, the word *here* (not 'there and here' as in the English translation) is mentioned seven times in this short passage, thus emphasizing that 'here' is where the happiest years of Galuzina's life took place. Each building, each window, each door come alive, full of memories for her. Just to close the cycle we come back to the place where we started:

> It was underneath this window that the puppy, Tomik, sat on his chain and yelped, so that you could hear him across the square in St. Helen Street (p. 282).

Galuzina's sentimental digressions into the past come suddenly to an end near the gray house when fragments of her thoughts are enclosed in *quotation marks*:

> "There they are in a pack, the *whole Sanhedrin*," thought Galuzina as she passed the grey house. "It's a den of filth and beggary." And yet, she reflected at once, her husband was wrong to hate the Jews so much. It's not as if they were the lords of the land, they were not important enough to affect Russia's destiny (p. 282).

And in *her own vocabulary, with her thoughts reeled back to the present*, she continues to search for an answer to the question that bothers her most—"What is the cause of the present misfortune?":

> Oh, but what nonsense was she wasting her time thinking about! Did they matter? Were they Russia's misfortune?... The towns were the trouble. Not that the country stood or fell by towns, but the towns were educated, and the country people had their heads turned...
> Or perhaps it was the other way round, perhaps ignorance was the trouble?—An educated man can see through walls, he can guess everything what happened

in advance, while the rest of us are like people in the dark wood. We only miss our hats when our heads have been chopped off... (p. 282).

In her typical language, dotted with folk sayings and proverbs, Galuzina is turning over in her mind the problems of the towns and the countryside, her country relatives and the events of her time. Finally, she feels as '[i]f weight has been lifted from her' and that '[i]t simply wasn't decent for a woman to be wandering about the streets so late' (p. 283) and she goes home. The reflections, however, offer more possibilities, as observed in the narrator's words following Galuzina's thoughts:

> Utterly confused by her reflections and having quite lost her thread of them, Galuzina went home. But before she went inside, she stood for a while in the porch, *going over a few more things in her mind* (p. 283).

These 'few more things' include people who are in her region on both sides of the civil war. Among them are old revolutionaries like Tiverzin, Antipov senior and others characters we meet later in the Forest Brotherhood. She thinks about them as follows:

> They had spent their lives dealing with machines and they were cold and merciless as machines themselves. They went about in sweaters and jerkins, they smoked through bone cigarette-holders and they drank boiled water for fear of catching something. Poor Vlas was wasting his time; these men would turn everything upside-down, they would always get their way (p. 283).

Galuzina's stream of consciousness ends with thoughts about herself and her position in her town and region. Her idiolect is confirmed in dialogue between her and

Ksyusha. Now, we can distinguish her vocabulary even better from the narrator's where quotation marks were omitted in her stream of consciousness.

The above passages and conclusions refer to Galuzina's thoughts as a stream of consciousness. Some readers see it as an internal dialogue or something else. I believe that the under-current of her thoughts is better understood when looking at the same type of stylization employed in conveying some of Yurii Zhivago's particular thoughts.

Like in the case of Galuzina, before describing Yurii's thoughts, the narrator writes about Yurii's surroundings. A detailed account of Zhivago's movements and activities is rendered. Before Yurii arrives at the stove where his stream of consciousness starts, he discovers that the wood he is using for the fire is marked with the letters 'K' and 'D,' indicating that they come from Varykino. That this kind of wood is found in Lara's apartment tells Yurii that it is supplied by Samdevyatov. Suspicions regarding a relationship between Samdevyatov and Lara start to bother Yurii. These feelings are conveyed in a symbolic, indirect way:

> The dry Kulabish logs crackled merrily and stormed into a blaze, and as they caught, Yurii's blind jealousy turned from the merest supposition into certainty (p. 350).

Having described Zhivago's movements and actions in great detail—not a characteristic device for the rest of the novel—the narrator penetrates Yurii's deliberations. Only after having described all possible nuances, does he turn to Zhivago's thoughts in the first person narrative. Thus, much like as he does in the case of Galuzina, the narrator first informs us about the background and the mental state of the protagonist and then writes:

He had no need to banish his suspicions; his mind leapt from subject to subject, and the thought of his family, flooding it again, submerged his jealous fantasies (p. 350).

'In Moscow! In Moscow!' The chapter begins with those words. Subsequently, all the information is given in a third person narrative. Having described the mental state of Yurii and the set-up, the author then brings us back to the initial situation:

So you are in Moscow, my dear ones? ... So you made all that long journey once again, and this time without me... I'll find you, even if I have to walk all the way to you. We'll see each other, we'll be together... Why doesn't the earth swallow me up, why am I such a monster that I keep forgetting that Tonya was to have another child and that she has surely had it! (p. 351).

Zhivago's stream of consciousness shows him tortured by his guilt towards his family, which brings him back to Lara, the cause of his guilt feelings. His reproach to Lara for not telling him anything regarding his family in the note she left him is now banded together with the reproach he feels for her not mentioning her relationship with Samdevyatov. This is the end of Zhivago's thoughts in the first person narration.

The narrator describes the decor of the room in which Yurii now finds himself. Zhivago's mental state is reflected in the way he sees the room. He suddenly feels like a stranger and superfluous in it. His thoughts, which follow—although not enclosed in quotation marks—do not leave any room for doubt regarding the voice, which clearly is Yurii's:

What a fool he had been to keep remembering this

house and missing it, what a fool to have come into this room, not as into an ordinary room but as if into the heart of his longing for Lara! How silly this way of feeling would seem to anyone outside! How different was the way strong, handsome, practical men, such as Samdevyatov, lived and spoke and acted! And why should Lara be expected to prefer his weakness and the dark, *obscure, unrealistic language of his love*? Did she need his turmoil? Did she herself wish to *be* that which she *meant* to him?

And what did she mean to him? Oh, that was easy! *He knew that perfectly well.*

A spring evening... the air is punctuated with scattered sounds. The voices of children playing in the street come from varying distances as if to show that the whole expanse is alive. The expanse is Russia, *his incomparable mother; famed far and wide, martyred, stubborn, extravagant, crazy, irresponsible, adored, Russia with her eternally splendid, disastrous and unpredictable gestures. Oh, how sweet it was to be alive! How good to be alive and love life! And how he longed to thank life, thank existence itself, directly, face to face, to thank life in person.*

This was exactly what Lara was. You could not communicate with life, but she was its representative, its expression, the gift of speech and hearing granted to inarticulate being.

And all that he has just reproached her with in the moment of confusion was a thousand times untrue. She was perfect and irreproachable (p. 351-352).

Here ends Yurii's stream of consciousness. The narrator takes over and describes his activities:

Tears of admiration and repentance filled his eyes. Opening the oven door, he poked the fire... Leaving the door open, he sat before the open flames, *delighting in the play of light and warmth on his face and hands.* The warmth and light brought him completely to his senses. He missed Lara unbearably and he longed for something which could bring him into touch with her at that very moment (p. 352).

The same fire that earlier symbolized the rage of jealousy, when Yurii suspected a relationship between Lara and Samdevyatov, now mirrors Yurii's love for Lara and his deeply loved mother Russia, affecting his thoughts and feelings.

As we progress, the roles are divided between the narrator and Zhivago in a way that the narrator deals with Zhivago's behaviour, and Zhivago's thoughts are in quotation marks.

The stream of consciousness ends with Yurii being in a good mood, satisfied with his relationship with Lara, and pleased with his family being back in Moscow. However, in the following section—the whole section—we read about Yurii Zhivago's dreams. These are the only dreams which are described at length in the novel. Since they are positioned as a continuation to the stream of consciousness, they too relate to Yurii's consciousness—more clearly evident if we pay attention to Yurii's observations in his diary regarding dreams:

> About dreams. It's usually taken for granted that you dream of something which has made a particularly strong impression on you during the day, but it seems to me just the contrary.
>
> Often it's something you paid no attention to at the time—a vague thought that you didn't bother to think out to the end, words spoken without feeling and which passed unnoticed—these are the things which return at night, clothed in flesh and blood as characters in dreams, as if to force you to make up for having neglected them in your waking hours (p. 257).

In his first dream Yurii sacrifices his son for an ill-conceived idea of honour and obligation vis-à-vis another woman (who is not the mother of his son). In the second dream the woman, for 'whom he has sacrificed all he had, whom he had preferred to everything, to a point that in comparison with her nothing had any value!' (p. 354), has no more time for him, has no longer any interest in him.

Two things can be deduced from Yurii's dreams: the pangs of conscience of a failed father and the fear of misunderstanding Lara's feelings for him. Lara is the essence of his life in his conscious and subconscious states of mind. If we remember the answer just one page earlier to 'what Lara meant to him,' we realize the large role Russia plays in Yurii's existence. For him Russia and Lara are both the essence of his life.

Thus, the appearance of the dreams soon after the stream of consciousness compliments his stream of consciousness with his subconscious mind—stressing the central role of consciousness in Zhivago's character, while also stressing the transcendental importance of the content conveyed through this form of narration.

Conclusion

Despite Galuzina and Zhivago being two completely different individuals belonging to different strata in Russian society, the content conveyed in the stylistic form of the stream of consciousness shows that at the essential level of existence Galuzina and Zhivago have much in common. In both cases, the stream of thought is built on the principle of association, each thought evolving from the preceding. For example, in Galuzina's case, as shown above, the mobilization orders which affect her son lead her thoughts to the war—the initial reason for the draft. The loss of the 'flower of Russia's manhood' she sees as a direct consequence of the war. This brings memories of better times, when she was a young maiden in her father's house. *Her own happy years are interwoven with Russia's happy years and this time belongs to the past.* Russia of her past appears in the places she is now walking. Among other things she is turning over in her thoughts is also her family's store, in which she spent the first years of her marriage. She then comes back to the present and the 'new' people connected with it. Galuzina's picture of Russia is a materialistic one. She thinks about the years Russia was progressing and prospering. Peasants and workers could move up in society, as her father did. In her picture of Russia, people at various levels of success were content with their place in life. When suddenly her mind turns to herself, she thinks of her own image the way she sees it and the way she is seen in Krestovozdvizhenks.

A similar logical connectedness in the stream of thoughts can be observed in Yurii Zhivago's mind.

In both cases Russia has a central place in their thoughts. *Russia's image in their thoughts is the reflection of what the ideal in life means to them.* For Galuzina, those are the years when she was bright, young and in demand—her own fate and Russia's fate blend and are traced to the same time. For Zhivago, the image of Lara and of Russia blends into one poetic vision of the beauty of life.

Common elements in their thoughts are jealousy and moments of confidence in themselves. Their individual perception of happiness agrees with their characters. Galuzina's world is materialistic, realistic, and her happiness is defined in those terms. Zhivago's world is poetic, idealistic, and his happiness rests in a world of these dimensions.

In the stylization of the stream of consciousness—the other end of the scale when compared to the skaz—the most personal, most vital thoughts of the characters are conveyed. In both cases, the attachment of their own lives with the life of Russia seems to be the dynamic power behind their way of living and seeing themselves. Russia is at the core of their being. Following the main principle of the novel, namely, *that content dictates the form*, what do we make of the content conveyed in the form of stream of consciousness? Obviously, a person's conscience is influenced by his Weltanschauung. A materialistic and idealistic point of view could coexist when love for Russia is shared by both. The content of this material has found its place in the stream of consciousness which emphasizes it best.

The author must have regarded of major importance the thoughts conveyed in the form of stream of consciousness, considering the well developed literary technique employed here. He gives a detailed *description of the conditions, the place, the time and the mood of the character before he proceeds with the stream of consciousness.* Then, in the first person narration of the character, *his or her style and vocabulary are established.* The character's discourse or thoughts are interrupted in order to describe the *place of the activity or external activities.* The author then recounts in third person, using the vocabulary of the narrator and the character, without separating the two with quotation marks. The latter phenomenon can be easily identified in the case of Galuzina, since her language differs clearly from the language of the narrator. In the case of Zhivago, however, it is more difficult to distinguish, since his style and vocabulary do not differ from those of the narrator, except for the fact that the narration in first versus third person differentiates between the two. It is obvious that the narrator identifies with Zhivago more than with any other character in the novel.

Prior to each instance of stream of consciousness the author alerts us that we are moving from speech to thoughts, while cautioning about their unpredictability regarding time and place. An instant in thoughts takes in years of one's life and is able to cover huge distances. While in the process of stream of consciousness the character stays in one place, as in the case of Zhivago, or is moving within a limited space, as in the case of Galuzina.

It warrants mentioning here that in chapter five of the novel, in section fifteen, Yurii Zhivago's thoughts are conveyed in a third person narration. The narrator communicates Zhivago's thoughts and reflects:

> His thoughts swarmed and whirled in the dark. They seemed to move in two main circles, two skeins which constantly tangled and untangled themselves (p. 148).

As Zhivago continues to think, the division into these two circles means separating events that took place in his life from old and new. Zhivago's thoughts about his personal destiny is closely connected to the destiny of Russia:

> This familiar circle also contained the foretaste of new things. In it were those omens and promises which before the war, between 1912 and 1914, had appeared in Russian thought, art and life, in the destiny of Russia as a whole and his own, Zhivago's (p. 148).

The connection of Zhivago's destiny to that of Russia—as shown in his thoughts here or in his stream of consciousness—is completely different from simple stories or fairytales. In the latter people become victims or heroes depending on external circumstances. It is also a very different connection from the one we can trace in the leader of the Forest Brotherhood or the other activists, including Strelnikov. All the latter are so busy with wanting to change life that they often forget about Russia and life itself. The idealistic relationship of Zhivago with Russia seems to be similar to that of the author with his country.

Point of View in the Novel

The titles of the chapters of the novel indicate their content and theme; they also communicate regarding structure. Thus, the title points to a way of reading the chapter and helps to locate certain information that otherwise could easily be missed. If we examine the method—the priom—which Pasternak employs to convey his message, we find that he follows the same principles which constitute the ideological leitmotif of the novel. The major theme of the novel is the conflict of the free individual with the constrictions of his freedom in the historic time in which he lives. The right of the individual to have his own opinion, be his own self, is constantly violated by the demands of the historic times described in the novel.

Didacticism is one of the main tools used in the spiritual war against the free individual. In the novel anti-didacticism is not only in the text but also shown in the method (priom) used to convey the text. A few examples from the novel show how this method works. The conflict between the free individual and the demands of the historic time is one of the leading themes of the novel. These are times when this conflict is intensified in the extreme by war, the revolution and the civil war. The freedom of the individual is discussed in the novel in different contexts including that of art. The protagonist, Yurii Zhivago, is searching for freedom in his profession as a physician, in his calling as a poet, and finally he expresses it in his art, his writing. The collection of his poetry, the last chapter of the novel, is completely free of the rhetoric and cliché so overwhelmingly powerful in his time. It is a model of free art written in the times when propaganda art prevailed.

Very few people manage to remain their own free selves during dynamic historical times as those described in the novel. The pressure of the times on the individual amplifies the isolation of those lone persons who do not think and act like the majority does. In seclusion in Varykino, when Zhivago examines through the prism of solitude concepts close to his heart, he rebels also against writers such as Gogol, Tolstoy and Dostoevsky, who were busy with 'such high-sounding matters' as 'ultimate purpose of mankind or their own salvation.' He believes that 'Gogol, Tolstoy and Dostoevsky worried and looked for the meaning of life and prepared for death and drew up balance sheets ...' (p. 259).

It is balance sheets, final conclusions and his own overt opinions as author that Pasternak refrains from in his method of writing.

Not only is the story of the novel saturated with anti-didacticism, but it is also expressed in the form the novel was written, in the very method it employed. It can be best observed in the *scattered nature of presenting a theme,* appearing in various chapters, far from one another, in the novel, *in the polyphony of voices* participating in the presentation of a theme, and in the *absence of a direct authorial voice.*

The scattered nature of presenting a theme frees the reader from the annoying didacticism the author is fighting against and gives more freedom to the reader's choice and interest. Thus, many themes are dispersed in the novel and are diffused in such a light impressionistic manner that without gathering and connecting them many readers may not notice them. This method is the antithesis of the annoying didacticism that filled the air in the period described in the novel and definitely is the antithesis of the writing of Socialist Realism that dominated Russian literature in the Soviet Union at the time the novel was written.

The polyphony of voices is mostly created by giving each individual his own voice, a particular way of thinking. Each voice belongs to a certain person and relates to a certain way of thinking which is not provoked by argument, but is in most cases the result of an individual point of view.

The author's voice, position or point of view, is absent at first glance. There is no authorial intervention, no intrusion into the main story; there is no authorial 'I,' no authorial commentary concerning the events or the people described in the novel. It would be injudicious to assign to the author the ideas of his heroes, since he often distances himself from them not only using a third person pronoun but also by alternating the use of the different forms of addressing a person in Russian, including the doctor title when speaking about Zhivago. The narrator does not explain his role. Thus, what is the narrator's connection to the story in the novel? He gives away that he belongs to the same era by several times running ahead of the time in the story, commenting on the weather, on nature and on events of a general nature. But the method the author employs, as revealed when carefully examined, makes it clear that *the strength of the authorial word is precisely in its absence.*

This paradox creates an irony outside the text that is nonverbal and instead compositional. The author's word reveals itself in the use of quotation marks and even more in their omission; it shows itself in the personal vocabulary and phraseology of the characters. The author avoids impersonal speech (thus stressing his idea of an independent individual), while stylistically highlighting the opposite of personal language, namely, the jargon of the time.

As was already mentioned, one of the main themes of the novel is the free individual and his own opinion and word. Later we will examine an example showing how the disappearance of individuality expresses itself in the inability to recognize the difference between one's own word and another's. The theme of the free individual and his characteristics are dispersed throughout the novel, as are many other themes. The theme of the free individual is shown by the author in the way he uses quotation marks. Hence we find that old Church Slavonic expressions in the text are in quotation marks, except those spoken by Mikulitsin, who is playing the role of a seminarist and therefore has appropriated them and made them part of his own language.

In the next passage from his 'Essay in an Autobiography,' Pasternak considers the old Church Slavonic vocabulary an important part of pre-revolutionary Russia:

For Block, Mayakovsky and Essenin pieces of church songs and readings were dear in their literal meaning, as segments of a way of life, along with the street, the home and any words of the colloquial language considering the next passage from his ' Essay in an Autobiography'.

Slavenisms are considered by the author to be a part of daily life, but by putting them in quotation marks he separates them from the thoughts and vocabulary of the characters who speak them. He does not put *Sovietisms* in quotation marks, in spite of the fact that in the new system, they, in a way, replaced the old Church Slavonic expressions. By not putting them in quotation marks, Pasternak shows that people use the new Soviet jargon, both expressions and words, as their own. The disappearance of individuality manifests itself in the inability to distinguish one's own word from the words of others (in this case, the Soviet propaganda).

In order to explain the 'scattered' method used in presenting issues, themes and characters in the novel, we will pay attention to some of its peculiarities. Let us look at such a secondary character as Panfil Palykh. As will become clear later, his first appearance in the novel is as an unknown soldier, who has shot and killed Gintz (chapter five, p. 144). The second time Panfil is mentioned (and is still not associated with the shooting), he appears, amongst other names, in Galuzina's stream of consciousness:

> All the same, it was the country people [our kinsmen the country people] who knew how to live. Look at her [our] relations, the Selvetins, Shelaburins, Panfil Palykh, the brothers Modykh. They relied on their own hands and their own heads, they were their own masters. The new farmsteads along the highway were a lovely sight. Fifteen dessiatins of arable land, sheep, horses, pigs and enough *corn in the barns for three years ahead*! And their farming machines! They even had harvesters! Kolchak was buttering them up, trying to get them on his side, and so were the commissars, to get them into the forest army. They had come back from the war with Georges Crosses and everyone was after them, wanting to employ them as instructors. Commissioned or not, if you knew your job you were always in demand. You could always find your feet (p. 282).

All that appears here about Panfil is in plural, about him and people of the same class. Galuzina sees Panfil as a man belonging to successful people. Those are people who are in 'demand' by both Kolchak and the forest commissars. He has enough corn for three years ahead. What will happen or has already happened to his grain we learned earlier in the novel—it will, eventually, be taken away from him (p. 212).

It is only when Panfil is mentioned for the third time, that it refers to him personally:

> "We have a case of it in the camp—Panfil Palykh, a former private in the Tsarist army, *a man with a high revolutionary consciousness and an innate class sense*. The cause of his trouble is his anxiety for his family in the event of him being killed and their falling into the hands of the Whites and being made to answer for him. It is a

very complex mentality ... I don't know Russian to question him properly. You could find out from Angelar or Kamenodvorsky. He ought to be examined" (p. 309).

This is how Kereny Lajos, a Hungarian communist, medical officer and prisoner of war, sees Palykh.
The fourth opinion about Palykh we get from the protagonist of the novel, doctor Yurii Zhivago:

"I know Palykh very well. At one time we often came across each other at army council meetings. *Dark and cruel, with a low forehead.* —I can't think what good you see in him. He was always for extreme measures, shooting and punishing. I have always found him repulsive. Still, I will take it up" (p. 309).

Doctor Zhivago believes that he knows Palykh well. Palykh's looks and personality are repulsive to him. He used to meet with Palykh at the army council; this leads us back to Meluzeevo, before the October Revolution, after the February Revolution, when there was still a promise of freedom.
The fifth person speaking about Panfil Palykh is Kamenodvorsky:

"Now another thing. It is a request from all of us. Will you have a look at a comrade of ours? ... *tried, tested, devoted to the cause and a splendid soldier.* There is something wrong with him."
"Palykh? Lajos told me."
"Yes. Go see him. Examine him."
"He is a mental case?"
"I suppose so. He says he has 'the creeps.' Hallucinations evidently. Insomnia. Headaches..."
"Where do I find Panfil?"

"You will find some commanders' tents in a clearing. We've put one of them at Panfil's disposal. He's got his family coming; they are in the convoy. That's where you will find him—in one of the tents—he's got battalion commander status—as a reward for revolutionary merit" (p. 311).

Judging by Kamenodvorsky's language and values, he joined the partisans for reasons different from those of Panfil's. His language is full of the stereotypical communist jargon, and his values are still not as arrogant as those of some other revolutionaries; he finds it necessary to justify the fact that Panfil was given a 'commander's tent' when he speaks to Zhivago. However, Pasternak comments here indirectly on the inequality—new social stratification—already existing among the partisans in the forest; people are again divided into 'classes,' just according to different criteria. It is hard not to remember 'We are all equal but some more equal than others' (George Orwell, *Animal Farm*).

The causes that lead to Panfil's 'merits' are presented in the plural and in several voices. This way it explains not only Panfil's status but it also makes him a representative of many others that are in the same category. Panfil belongs to the class of people who were 'active' in the beginning of the revolution, which makes Panfil a man 'with an innate class consciousness' and a man who deserves a special position in the new class hierarchy.

Before we hear Panfil's story about himself, the narrator summarizes the historical events that lead to the status Panfil enjoys in the camp:

When, at the beginning of the revolution, it had been feared that, as in 1905, the upheaval would be an abortive event affecting only the educated few and leaving the deeper layers of society untouched, everything possible has been done to spread revolutionary propaganda among the people to disturb them, stir them up and lash them into fury.

In those early days, men like Panfil, who needed no encouragement to hate intellectuals, officers and gentry with a savage hatred, were regarded by enthusiastic left-wing intellectuals as a great find and were greatly valued. Their inhumanity seemed a marvel of 'class consciousness,' their barbarism a model of proletarian firmness and revolutionary instinct. By such qualities Panfil has established his fame and he was held in great esteem by partisan chiefs and party leaders (p. 315).

The above speaks for itself. The order in which the facts about Panfil are presented shows that the social stratification which already exists in the forest, has started even earlier. In this context, all the adjectives used to describe Panfil by Dr. Lajos and Kamenodvorsky point to the new value system by which the revolutionary society already lives. The summary of the historical situation that leads to the present day value system and its jargon tells in a matter-of-fact manner how it happened. However, the above descriptions gain an even more poignant meaning when the voice of Panfil himself is added to the polyphony.

It is a long story. The way he tells it reminds us of a folk tale, or even a fairytale, in both vocabulary and in form. He is interrupted several times by Doctor Zhivago who comes to see him as requested by the commander. Panfil addresses Zhivago as 'Comrade Army Doctor' and tells him about himself. He starts the story as follows:

> "They say a tale is soon told. But my story is a long one. I couldn't tell it all in three years. I don't know where to begin.
>
> "Well, I will try. My wife and I. We were young. She looked after the house. I worked in the fields. It

was not a bad life. We had children. They took me for the army. They sent me to the war. Well, the war. What should I tell you about the war? You have seen it, Comrade Doctor— then the revolution came. I saw the light. The soldier's eyes were opened. We heard that it wasn't only the foreigners who were enemies. We had enemies at home too. 'Soldiers of world revolution, down your rifles, go home, turn against the bourgeois!' And so on. You know it yourself Comrade Army Doctor. Well, to go on. Then came the civil war. I joined the partisans. Now I'll have to leave out a lot or I'll never end" (p. 315).

This part of Panfil's story, actually, gives in his own words and from his point of view the same historical facts as voiced by the narrator and found in Galuzina's thoughts. Further, Panfil speaks about the lost war of the partisans and about his suffering caused by his worries regarding the fate of his wife and children should they fall into the hands of the enemy:

"He's beating us, the White bastard. Anyway, it isn't me we are talking about. I'm done for. I will soon be dead. But I can't take the little ones with me into the next world, can I? They will stay and they will fall into his heathen hands. He'll squeeze the blood out of them drop by drop" (p. 316).

But it turns out that Panfil has still not told the doctor the main reason for 'the creeps' he is suffering from. To Zhivago's question he responds:

"Well, doctor. I haven't told you everything. I have kept back the most important thing. Now, I'll tell you the whole truth if you want it, I will say to your face but you mustn't hold it against me.

"I've done away with lot of your kind, there's a lot of officers' blood on my hands. Officers, gentry. And it never worried me. Spilt it like water. Names and numbers all gone out of my head. But there is one little fellow I can't get out of my mind; I killed that brat and I can't forget it. Why did I have to kill him? He made me laugh, and I killed him for a joke, for nothing like a fool ... Well that's the reason I got the creeps. I dream about that station at night. At the time it was funny. Now I'm sorry" (pp. 316-317).

Panfil's story brings the doctor back to Melyuzeyevo:

"Was that at Biryuchi station near the town of Melyuzeyevo?"
"Can't remember."
"Were you in the Zibushino rising?"
"Can't remember."
"Which front were you on? Was it the western front? Were you in the west?"
"Somewhere like that. It could have been in the west. I can't remember" (p. 317).

One has to remember the episode that took place two hundred pages earlier in order to connect to it the story told now by Panfil from his point of view. The first time the episode was conveyed by the narrator in third person. Now the story is told by Panfil and we have a face for the murderer of Gintz. Even Panfil understands that he killed Gintz for no good reason. The senselessness of murdering Gintz is now confirmed by the murderer himself.

Panfil's story concludes only in the following chapter. We get a description of Panfil in his family circle:

Panfil was devoted to all of them and loved his children to destruction. He surprised Yurii by his skill in carving toy rabbits, cocks and bears for them, using the corner of his finely sharpened axe blade (p. 323).

Further we find out from the words of his wife, when she asks for help from Kubarikha, that she is afraid for his well-being: "I'm afraid he'll do away with himself" (p. 329). Just a few pages further we read:

In desperate anguish—to prevent their future suffering, and to end his own—he killed them himself, *felling his wife and his three children with the same razor-sharp axe which he used to carve toys for the two little girls and the boy who had been his favorite* (p. 334).

Panfil's story ends with him losing his mind and 'No one was sorry for him' (p. 334).

All the above quoted excerpts show Panfil Palykh in the light of historical events. All of the voices—of Galuzina, Lajos, Zhivago, Kamenodvorsky, Panfil, his wife—speak of Panfil's situation from their own point of view, naming some of the same facts and events in their own words. There is also the matter-of-fact voice of the narrator among these voices. His voice conveys the killing of Gintz and the historical data at the beginning of the October Revolution. The author's commentary, as well as polemics of different opinions, is absent. Their absence triggers the desire for a heated discussion, for a discussion which is outside the printed text. The role of the reader in these polemics is conditioned by his or her range of knowledge and interest in the real historical facts that led to and existed in the Soviet state.

This method of presenting historical facts by individual voices coming from different social strata of society shows the tragedy of human fate when it falls into the whirlwind of historical events.

Concerning the 'scattered' nature of the theme and the polyphony of voices, we find in the critical literature about the novel a negative opinion. Unfortunately, critics did not make an effort to bring together even the basic information concerning a character. More importantly, they did not even consider that this 'scattered' presentation of information is not accidental but indeed intentional. The novel deals with war, revolution and civil war, and the author confines himself to scant presentations in the spirit of the excerpts quoted above. He is reproached, while writing about historical events, for not describing mass scenes like Tolstoy did.

Gladkov reproaches Pasternak for the absence of conflict in the novel:

> The influence of Dostoevsky can be noticed, but in Dostoevsky's work his dialogues-arguments are serious disputes with dialectical equality of the arguing sides (as shown outstandingly by Bakhtin in his book), and in *Doctor Zhivago* all the acting characters are little Pasternak's, only one is mixed up thicker, the other more watery.

Precisely the absence of expressed conflict among the voices, the absence of opinions and the absence of 'dialectical equality' as well as the absence of polarized arguments, is not due to a 'mistake' by the author. It is a method deliberately chosen by him to *convey the content not only in words but also through the method of presentation.*

This method lets the reader's personality and his or her point of view take on an active role in the reading of this novel. *The scattered nature of presentation used in the description* of themes and characters frees the novel from didacticism, against which the whole content of the novel is directed. It may be why the novel was written. The anti-didacticism in the text, in adhering to the same principle, is also conveyed in a scattered form.

The indicated peculiarities (scattered method of

description, the polyphony of voices, absence of conflict and argument, absence of an overt vocal opinion by the author) are typical in the portrayal of other characters as well. Even when more voices are participating in the depiction of the main characters, the method used is the same.

In the preceding pages we quoted excerpts showing Panfil's behaviour in his family circle and then in the killing of his wife and children. In this study the lines referring to the axe are italicized. All that is said about it is that 'he killed them himself, *felling his wife and his three children with the same razor-sharp axe which he used to carve toys for the two little girls and the boy who had been his favorite*' (p. 334).

This tells us that in the hands of Panfil the same tool creates and destroys. This symbolism applies not only to Panfil's life, but also to the lives of many other people with a similar background and fate. Before the war Panfil Palykh farmed his land, he loved his work and his family. After the war he applied the same zeal to destruction that he applied before to his farming, which emphasizes the danger of tools in the hands of people who do not think on their own. As a symbol it is carried to the extreme of self-destruction, representing the results of the revolution and the civil war.

When discussing the method used in the novel, however, it is more than the symbolical use of the axe. What is important to remember is that this entire message is expressed in only a few words and it is never mentioned in the novel again. The symbolical weight in the novel is major, belying the fact that it is drawn in such light strokes that at first reading much of it may be missed.

It is precisely with these subtle notes that the author comments not loudly enough to be heard by all, but on those who notice their effect is not lost.

◆ ◆ ◆

Now let us see how this same above-mentioned

technique is used to deal with an episode. In chapter ten, among other things, the episode is described of the drafting into the army by the Whites. We already know that Kolchak's government is in power in the region, and that it is the latest of several successive governments, alternating between the Reds and the Whites.

The first appearance of the conscription theme is very symbolical if one is to see both conceptually and literally *the point of view* from which the conscription is perceived:

> To the small boys who had climbed up the belfry to watch the bell-ringers, the houses below looked like small white boxes jumbled close together. *Little black people, hardly bigger than dots,* walked in front of houses and stopped in front of them. They stopped to read the decree calling up three more age groups (p. 278).

Who is looking and from where, the size of the people observed—all this presents here figuratively the theme of conscription. For example, we see the size of a person in front of history, and hence in front of the conscription, followed by the conscription from the point of view of Galuzina—a mother, whose son is subject to this draft:

> But this was not the chief cause of her worry. *The mobilization order posted up that day affected her poor, silly boy, Teryoshka.* She tried to drive the thought of it from her head, but the white patches in the darkness were there to remind her at every turn (p. 279).

While at first we have seen the declarations about the conscription through the eyes of the unconcerned, far distanced by location and age (little boys), now we are looking at it with the eyes of a mother whose only son is affected by this mobilization. She perceives it as 'mortal peril' (p. 280) to her son. In her thoughts things connected with the conscription are the war, the revolution, the civil war. In her thoughts the draft becomes the first step in the losses of lives and the disaster that happened to her country.

The next time the conscription is mentioned, the results of the declarations are celebrated:

> In Kuteiny a farewell party was being given for the new recruits conscripted by Kolchak ... Tables spread with food and drink for the recruits stood under the open sky in Kuteiny ... The villagers had pooled their resources to provide the entertainment (p. 291).

Next follows the speech of Vlas Galuzin, Teryoshka's father. The speech earns both the compliments and the suspicions of Teryoshka's friends: "He is certainly a fine fellow! But I suppose it's not for nothing he's working so hard. I suspect he will get you off conscription as a reward" (p. 292). Their suspicion has no justification. Earlier in her thoughts, Galuzina reproached her husband thinking that:

> Vlas was gallivanting up and down the highway, making speeches to the new recruits, exhorting them to mighty feats of arms. Instead of looking after his own son, the fool, and saving him from his mortal peril! (p. 280).

A commotion and misunderstanding occur and, as a result, Teryoshka and two of his friends are forced to run to the forest to the partisans until they sort things out here. The reasons for the commotion, the conversation between Teryoshka and his friends and the following quote, treat with irony the situation of the civil war, in particular the commanding parties on both sides. Again, it is only a concise commentary on the politicized situation in the country and it tells us how disassembled the whole division is:

> The young men had nothing on their conscience and it

was foolish of them to hide: most of them ran away on the spur of the moment, because they were drunk and had lost their heads. A few, however, had kept company which now seemed to them compromising and might, they were afraid, lead to their undoing if it were known. It was true that their friends were nothing worse than hooligans, but you never knew: anything might have a political angle nowadays. Hooliganism was considered a sign of black reaction in the Soviet zone, while in the White zone it regarded as bolshevism (p. 294).

The conscription theme is concluded in an ironical tone; the son of Vlas Galuzin, who worked for the conscription of soldiers to fight the partisans, is forced, because of pointless divisions, to join the partisans.

In the presentation of this *event*, the same method is used as the one before in portraying a *character*. It is also used later in presenting the central *theme* of the novel.

The same phenomenon seen from different points of view, absence of argument or discussion among them, *absence of a direct opinion expressed by the author,* everything conveyed in a scattered form—mean completely avoiding didacticism. This objective presentation of the event underlines the tragedy of the civil war. The conscription, the source supplying the fighting soldiers, without which no war is possible, figures here as the centre of the event. It is seen differently by various people, e.g., 'little people,' all people are like little dots in the vortex of the civil war.

Describing people the size of a dot is figurative: this is their 'size' in history. However, along with this symbolism, although depicted in but a few strokes, we have here also the human measure of the conscription—the feelings of a mother for her only son.

As already emphasized earlier, the main theme of the novel is the free individual and his conflict with the historical time. A free individual has his own opinion. He is able to express it in his own words. A free individual is able to separate his words from the words of others. In order to show this, Pasternak opens the novel with a passage, with a rhythm of a poem that illustrates the attention he has paid to the *semantics of the word in the novel:*

> Passers-by made way for the procession, *counted the wreaths* and *crossed themselves.* Some joined in out of curiosity and asked: "Who is being buried?"—"Zhivago," they were told.—"Oh, I see. That explains it."—"It isn't him. It's his wife."—"Well, it comes to the same thing. *May she rest in peace.—It's a fine [rich] funeral"* (p. 13).

Two common human characteristics—*being in awe in front of death* and *being in awe in front of riches*—are shown in action and in words, *in action:* crossed themselves, counted the wreaths, *in words*: may she rest in peace, a rich funeral. A few pages further on, we find another example of how the meaning of the word is defined by the context. It is presented in a short conversation taking place between Nikolay Nikolayevich Vedenyapin and Pavel. It shows also how the social category of a person is expressed in very few words:

> *"Are those landlords' or peasants' fields?"* Nikolay Nikolayevich asked Pavel, the publisher's odd-job man who sat sideways on the box, shoulders hunched and legs crossed to show that driving was not his regular job.
> *"These are the masters' "* Pavel lit his pipe, drew on it and after silence jabbed with the end of his whip in another direction; *"And those are ours!"* (pp. 15-16).

What to Nikolay Nikolayevich is the 'landlords' and the 'peasants' to Pavel it is the 'masters' and 'ours.' Pavel translates the words of Nikolay Nikolayevich into his social idiolect. Although he is the publisher's odd-job man and does not farm the land anymore, the peasant's land to him is still 'ours' and the landlords are his 'masters.'

In this example the author shows how the social classification of a person is reflected in the choice of few words, only two in each case.

These two examples above, appearing already in the very beginning of the novel, show that in his novel, like in his poetry, the word can be charged with additional inference. These examples show the extra semantic and symbolical meaning that can be found in the text.

The next example defines two different personalities and, again, in very few words:

"The *vital nerve* of the problem of poverty," Nikolay Nikolayevich read from the revised manuscript.

"Essence would be better, I think," said Ivan Ivanovich, making the correction on the galleys.

"On the other hand, the statistics of births and deaths show," dictated Nikolay Nikolayevich.

"Insert, 'for the year under review'," said Ivan Ivanovich and made a note (p. 17).

Further on in the conversation between Nikolay Nikolayevich and Ivan Ivanovich we learn about their different Weltanschauung (world view) and their way of expressing it. Vedevyapin's gift of eloquence is repeatedly shown in their conversation as is Voskoboynikov's pedantry in his short remarks.

The above examples show the attention given to the word, to its dialogical and symbolical weight. Later we find in the novel several passages connecting the individual's word with his or her opinion and relation to freedom. This is how it is summed up by Lara:

It was then that falsehood [untruth] came into our Russian land. The great misfortune, *the root of all the evil to come, was the loss of faith in the value of personal opinion.* People imagined that it was out of date to follow their own moral sense, *that they all must sing the same tune in chorus, and live by other people's notions, the notions that were crammed down everybody's throat.* And there arose the *power of the glittering phrase*, first the *tsarist* then *revolutionary* (p. 363).

This quotation has something in common with Zhivago's remark concerning his former friends:

His friends had become strangely dim and colourless. Not one of them had kept their own outlook, his/her own world ...
But how quickly, once the lower classes had risen and the rich had lost their privileges, had these people faded! How effortlessly, how happily, *had they given up the habit of independent thought*—which at this rate could never in fact have been genuinely theirs!
The only people with whom Yurii now felt at home were Tonya, her father and two or three of his colleagues, people in plain, ordinary jobs who got on with them decently and modestly (p. 160).

It is clear to Lara that 'falsehood' comes when people who have their own opinion vanish and are replaced with those who 'sing the same tune in the chorus'. A person without his or her own opinion propagates 'falsehood.' The ' glittering phrase' replaces the individual's word or opinion. And once it is a phrase, it is not even important whose phrase it is, tsarist or revolutionary—what's important is that it is 'falsehood' and therefore it constitutes the loss of one's own opinion, one's own word. Yurii loses interest in what his friends have to say to him when they lose their own opinions;

even worse, he cannot be part of this society:

> "What is it that prevents me from being useful as a doctor or a writer? I think it's not so much our privations or our wanderings or our constantly changing and unsettled lives, as the *power in our day of rhetoric, of the cliché—all this 'dawn of the future', 'building a new world', 'torchbearers of mankind'"* (p. 258).

As can be seen from the above, it is not the hardships in his life that prevent Zhivago from working as a doctor or from writing; it is his inability to get used to, or accept, the rule of the rhetoric and the cliché of his time. For Zhivago, like for Lara, a cliché phrase is falsehood. The loss of one's own opinion and word and the repetition of meaningless phrases mean not to be true to oneself, mean inability to create, work or go on with one's life; they mean the end of one's life. The novel shows that the last stage in losing individuality occurs when a person, with utmost sincerity and the best of efforts, can no longer regain his own opinion or voice, or, indeed, even recognize his own voice anymore. This is clearly expressed in the following passages:

> Dudorov had recently come back from his *first term of deportation*; *his civil rights had been restored* to him and he was allowed to resume his research and his lectures at the university.
> Now he was confiding to his friends his feelings and his state of mind in exile. His comments were not influenced by cowardice or by any external consideration. [He spoke to them *sincerely and not hypocritically*, AM.]
> He was saying that the arguments of the prosecution, his treatment in prison and after he came out, and particularly his heart-to-heart talks with the interrogator, *'ventilated his brains,' 're-educated him*

150

politically,' opened his eyes to many things he has not seen before and made him *'grow in stature as a person'.*

These reflections appealed to Gordon just because they were so *hackneyed.* He nodded his head with sympathy and agreed with Dudorov in everything. It was the very triteness of Dudorov's feelings and expressions that moved him most; *he took the textbook orthodoxy of his sentiments to be the sign of their common humanity.*

Dudorov's pious platitudes were in the spirit of the age (pp. 430-431).

In the above excerpts we see the loss of individuality carried to its extreme. Here a sincere and honest person becomes the *voice of someone else's spirit —the spirit of his age.* Dudorov does not recognize anymore his own voice, his own opinion. He is not aware how he promotes somebody else's opinion as his own! Gordon listens to him and agrees with him in everything, because, like Dudorov, he does not have an opinion of his own. Zhivago sees hypocrisy in their behaviour, but in order not to quarrel with them he no longer tells them what he thinks. He just concludes in his thoughts: 'Men who are not free always idealize their bondage' (p. 431).

A. Gladkov asserts that, unlike in Dostoevsky's works, there are no 'dialogues-arguments,' or 'serious disputes' with 'dialectical equality.' What we have here is *an inequality between the spirit of the age and the free individual!*

In the conversation between friends, Dudorov uses *words of the Soviet jargon* implanted in him by the system. He cannot differentiate between his own word and the Soviet phrases inculcated in him by the regime.

Pasternak conveys Dudorov's speech in the third person, showing that using expressions like *'re-educated him politically,' 'first term of deportation'* and *'his civil rights have been restored'* is by now a natural part of Dudorov's own vocabulary and expressions. The author does not use quotation marks or other means to underline their novelty in his vocabulary. On the contrary, he establishes their place in contemporary parlance by bringing to the reader's attention that Gordon liked them precisely because of their triteness.

Both Gordon and Dudorov belong to a certain *type of people*. They belong to to *'good university circles'*—the new intelligentsia. Belonging to a type, as mentioned earlier in the novel, deprives them of their individuality:

> "It's a good thing when a man is different from the image of him. It shows *he isn't a type*. If he were it would be *the end of him as a man*. But if you can't place him in a category, it means that at least part of him is what a human being is ought to be. *He has a grain of immortality"* (p. 268).

Belonging to a certain type is the end of a person, his condemnation. If he cannot be placed in any category, if he does not stand out, he embraces his freedom and true humanity.

The free individual is associated with concept of immortality in several places in the novel and in connection with several characters. Regarding the above quote, the author again uses the method of scattering the material. We find words relating to immortality already in the first line of the novel, "On they went, singing 'Eternal Memory'." As we will see later, the concept of immortality is connected with the concept of eternal memory in the context of the history of mankind. History here means 'centuries of systematic work devoted to the solution of the enigma of death, so that death itself may eventually be overcome' (p. 18). According to Nikolay Nikoloyevich, 'spiritual equipment' for such work is in the Gospels.

> Firstly, the 'love for one's neighbour—the supreme form of living energy' are the two concepts which ... are

the main part of the makeup of modern man—without them he is *inconceivable—the idea of free personality* and of life regarded as a sacrifice (p. 19).

According to Nikolay Nikolaevich's philosophy, the free individual is at the centre of the universe, thus giving him the place that prior to Christianity belonged to peoples and gods.

"And then, into this tasteless heap of gold and marble, He came, light-footed and clothed in light, with his marked humanity, his deliberate Galilean provincialism, and from that moment there were *neither gods nor peoples,* there was *only man*—man the carpenter, man the ploughman, man the shepherd ... man whose name does not sound in the least proud but who is sung in lullabies and portrayed in picture galleries the world over" (p. 49).

Simushka, a follower of Nikolay Nikolaevich, interprets his theories in her own words and in them too we discover the special order she ranks the free individual:

Something in the world had been changed. Rome was at an end. The reign of numbers was at an end. The duty, imposed by armed force to live unanimously as a people, as a whole nation, was abolished. Leaders and nations belonged to the past. They were replaced by *the doctrine of personality and freedom* (p. 370).

Although Sima speaks mostly from a religious point of view, and she and her sisters are with the revolution, the parallel she draws between Rome and the present brings us back to the main theme of the novel—the conflict between the free personality and his time. She does not stop there, but brings in a few more details from the present, to make sure that Lara understands her teaching in the context of the times. Stressing that 'this is a small digression,' she mentions the following:

> In everything to do with the care of the workers, the protection of the mothers, the struggle against the power of money, our revolutionary era is a wonderful era of new, lasting, permanent achievements. But in its interpretation of life and the philosophy of happiness which it preaches—it's simply impossible to believe that it is meant to be taken seriously, it's such a comical remnant of the past. If all this *rhetoric* about *leaders* and peoples had power to reverse history, it would set us back thousands of years to the Biblical times of shepherd tribes and patriarchs ... (p. 371).

Her full 'lecture' and the above quotes show that for her the highest preaching of Christ converges to the free individual. However, beyond religion, Sima is not indifferent to what is happening in the country now. Although she and her sister welcomed the revolution, by drawing a parallel between Rome and what is happening in Russia now, she shows what is happening to the ideal of the free individual at the present time. In her philosophy Sima does not connect the *free individual* with immortality, but she sees him as the *highest achievement of mankind* and the most recent.

Yurii Zhivago, brought up and educated by Nikolai Nikolaevich (and not only on books) and schooled in the natural sciences, sees immortality as the memory of oneself that one leaves with other people:

> You in others are yourself, your soul. This is what you are. This is what your consciousness has breathed and lived on and enjoyed throughout your life—your soul, your *immortality*, your life in others. And what now? You have always been in others and you will remain in

others. And what does it matter to you if later on it is called your memory? This will be you—the you that enters the future and becomes a part of it (p. 70).

The closest connection between the concept of individuality and immortality is represented by Yurii Zhivago's collection of poems. They contain all the above themes. Without considering the details of style and content, it is evident that they are completely free of the lofty phrases—as well as of the jargon and themes—of his days. In his poems the writer presents the free individual, free from the influences of the times. There is nothing in his poems of the ideas and jargon that rule his times. The poet is free and he promotes ideas of a free individual. Like in the novel as a whole, the poet conveys his ideas just by the timbre of his voice—a free, independent one, uninfluenced by the voices of his time. No attention is paid to those other voices.

Hamlet and Christ share the fate of self sacrifice. *The idea of life as a sacrifice* appears in the first and last poem of the collection. Pasternak understood Hamlet's role differently from the one conventionally adopted:

> From the moment of the appearance of the ghost, Hamlet ceases to live for himself, in order to 'fulfill the will of the one who delegated him.' Hamlet is not a drama of lack of character, but a drama of *duty and self renunciation* (From an introduction to the school edition of Pasternak's translation of Hamlet.)

To 'fulfill the will of the one who delegated him' is a motif that appears in the first and last poem of the collection, and is also expressed in similar words to stress its importance.

In the poem 'Hamlet':
"Abba, Father, if it be possible:
Let this cup pass from me."

In 'Gethsemane':
"Sweating blood, he prayed to his Father,
That this cup of death should pass him by."

According to the story of the novel, Zhivago's poems serve as a source of hope for and trust in the future for his friends who did not understand Yurii while he was alive and therefore did not appreciate him at the end of his life. The historical time when these poems were written are described in the novel. Those were times that did not allow even a minimum of freedom and independence for the individual. Those were times when people like Yurii Zhivago were seen as fallen, lost and not needed by anyone and as lone persons, because they did not join the mainstream of the time. *This is the reason that these poems, free of ideas and themes prevalent in the poet's time, free of the jargon and phraseology of that age, are such an important document regarding the free individual.* The personal style of the poet in those poems, as a contrast to the ruling phrases and slogans of his time, connects here *the idea of the free individual* with his own 'word' in the most obvious and convincing way. The personality of the poet is characterized here by his ideas and in his words. His perception of the world is completely his own and is totally clear of the spirit of his time.

Thus, the last chapter of the novel, consisting of Yurii Zhivago's poems, sums up the idea of the free individual, which plays a principal role in the thematics of the novel. The method and the tone of the summary do not differ from those employed in the novel, where the life of the author of these poems is presented. The argument with the era, loud voices, so typical of those times, are absent in his poems.

The quoted passages have shown how this theme is dispersed throughout the novel. It is evident from the above that even the idea of the free individual—the leitmotif of the novel—is dispersed throughout the text just to avoid didacticism even as concerns the main theme. Thus, as already mentioned, the very method the author employs to convey the content in itself imparts an important aspect of the content; indeed, it complements the verbal content and reinforces its expression.

In the poem 'August' the poet describes his own funeral and in four lines sums up his life and his creativeness:

Goodbye to the span of outstretched wings
Free stubbornness of flight,
Image of the world revealed in speech [word] (AM)
Creativeness, working of miracles (p. 487).

In truth, the content and the tone of these poems, written in the described Soviet times, are close to the realm of miracles.

It is not unusual to find a connection between content and form in well written works; however, here the method, priom, is more than a connection; it is an integral part of the content. When the principle which the method follows here is to avoid a summary interpretation, it becomes contradictory to make one in the case of this novel. Yet, for greater clarity, we will attempt to summarize the way in which the free individual is presented in the above-mentioned examples.

In the first two examples attention is drawn to the semantic and dialogic features the word commands in the novel. Thus, the background to the word in the concept of the free individual is prepared. The third example deals with the connection between literary style and the individual. Next, the connection between the free individual and his word and opinion are shown. Further, a total loss of individuality is defined, a loss of a person's own word and opinion, resulting in an inability to distinguish between his own speech (language) and that of the other. Finally, in conclusion, Pasternak notes that, in contrast, in ultimate fulfillment, the reward for loyalty to one's own individuality is eternal memory and immortality.

The poems at the end of the novel are documentary proof of the victory of the free individual over his times and warrant his immortality and eternal memory.

In order to discover the free individual in this collection of poems, all the above aspects of the word need to be examined. In this part of the work we discussed the point of view of the author. In the three examples discussed, the position of the author is the same, in spite of the fact that three different concepts are viewed. In all those essentially different examples we find that the method the author uses remains faithful to the same principles that were discussed earlier, namely, *dispersion of the theme,* which frees us from importunate didacticism, *the polyphony of voices* without confrontation and argument and *absence of conclusions as well as of the author's voice as such.* The protest against didacticism voiced in the text is also practiced in the method used to convey it.

The time in which Yurii Zhivago lives demands from the individual full capitulation. This is how it is presented in his own words:

> It's the common illness of our time. I think its causes are chiefly moral. The great majority of us are required to live a life of constant, systematic duplicity. Your health is bound to be affected if, day after day, you say the opposite of what you feel, if you grovel before what you dislike and rejoice at what brings you nothing but misfortune (pp. 431-432).

Physically, Yurii Zhivago is conquered. Destroyed by the system, he dies at a young age. But the violence his soul has suffered does not appear in his voice—his poems. However the protest of Yurii Zhivago against violating the freedom of the individual is well conveyed in the novel and in the poems that conclude it.

Sources

In English
Boris Pasternak
Doctor Zhivago
Collins Harwill
1988

In Russian
Boris Pasternak
Doctor Zhivago
Ann Arbor: University of Michigan Press, 1958

(....AM) —When translated by author.

Printed in Great Britain
by Amazon